The Symington factories, an engraving from the company prospectus, 1898.

foundations of Fashion

by Philip Warren

Designed by Central Design Section
Leicestershire County Council

Printed & produced by Polar Print, Leicester

ISBN 0 85022 4365

Foreword

Cover photograph: c1890.
Red and black sateen, straight front corset.
Museum ref. B50

The fashion industry plays an important part in the history of Leicestershire. At the heart of the East Midlands, Leicestershire has traditionally been the home of new developments in the mass manufacturing and distribution of clothing. Knitwear, hosiery, footwear, lace and foundation garment production have all developed from small workshops to mass production industries over a period of four hundred years. Today Leicestershire is home to the international fashion retailer Next.

The Symington collection has long been regarded as important not only to local people but also to many thousands of designers, researchers, students and enthusiasts from across the world. Over the forty years that the collection has been made public, at Symington's own museum in Market Harborough and, since 1980, through Leicestershire Museums Service, it has developed an international reputation for its quality and diversity.

Because of the fragile nature of historic costume and textiles there can be no permanent display of the Symington collection. A series of exhibitions and temporary displays, along with loans of material to exhibitions in Britain, the United States, Australia and Europe has meant that the fascinating garments, tools, artwork and photographs that form the collection have been made widely available. Researchers and students can access the collection for close and detailed study and this publication acts as an introduction to the collection for them, and as a general source of information for others.

The value of museum collections is not only the objects and artefacts themselves, but in the rich accumulation of associated information, archives and recorded memories. This unique resource has the potential to inspire, delight and educate present and future generations and help create a picture of the changing lives of Leicestershire people throughout history. The Symington collection has been shaped, influenced and enhanced by many people and I would like to thank all those who have contributed to it, from volunteers to those who have raised awareness of the collection internationally.

Thanks must go to the Courtaulds group, who generously donated the original collection in 1980 and made a subsequent gift of material in 1990. It was Patrick Boylan, Director of Leicestershire Museums in 1980, who had the vision to recognise the cultural value of the collection and who worked tirelessly for it to stay together and in Leicestershire. Colleagues at Harborough District Council must be thanked for their support of the Symington legacy. My personal thanks go to designer Ian Jones and particularly to Philip Warren, Keeper of Cultural Life, for his dedication to the Symington collection and to seeing this splendid publication to fruition.

Heather Broughton

Head of Leicestershire Museums,
Arts and Records Service

Contents

Introduction

"Without proper foundations there can be no fashion"

- Christian Dior

This is the story of a small family firm that developed into an international concern and at its height helped many millions of women achieve the fashionable figure of the day.

In May 1980 R. & W.H. Symington & Co. of Market Harborough, with the agreement of the main board of the Courtaulds Group, presented the Symington Collection to Leicestershire County Council's Museums, Arts and Records Service. Since that time the collection, which contains nearly 1,300 garments, has been a unique and valuable resource for students of technology, fashion, social history and gender studies.

Mr Christopher Page, the curator of the collection until 1980 did much to catalogue, date and interpret the thousands of garments, photographs, pictures, tools, advertising ephemera and company papers that make up the collection. They were the legacy of a company with a history stretching back for over a hundred years. Christopher's enthusiasm for the collection and his loyalty to the company were celebrated in the first exhibition of the collection in 1981, but unfortunately his untimely death at the end of 1980 meant that he never saw his text for the catalogue published to accompany the display. Since the initial gift the final phase of production from 1980 to 1990 has been added to the collection, completing the Symington story.

The garments and their supporting advertisements give us an insight into the development of corsetry, foundation garments and swimwear from the late nineteenth century through to beginning of the 1990s. They include not only corsets made by R. & W.H. Symington, but also pieces made by competitors from all over the world. The company excelled in the production of corsetry for a mass market and its success included the manufacture of styles similar to other companies but at a far cheaper price.

While the collection is extensive it is also selective. It tells the story of one company's business practice over a period of one hundred and thirty years and does not pretend to be a comprehensive history of corsetry and underwear. The production techniques described in this book refer to those at the Market Harborough factory and should not be taken as a universal view of corsetry making.

The garments illustrated here are a selection of some of the more interesting examples in the collection, or have been chosen because they illustrate a typical style reflecting a general fashion trend. New material from the advertising archive has been specially photographed for this publication but the black and white corsetry photographs are those taken for the original catalogue of 1981. As good black and white photographs already existed it was decided that these very fragile and early corsets should not be put onto forms and photographed.

Each garment is supported with a detailed caption of technical, design and manufacturing information. The introduction to each section briefly describes the changes in fashion and society and how the company responded to the challenges of each new period.

For the first time the growing collection of recorded memories of some of the Symington workforce has been used to illustrate its history.

Garments from the collection have been included in exhibitions in museums all over the world and a selection of corsets are displayed alongside the Museum Service's collection of fashionable dress. The rest of the collection is stored as a research and study resource, which is in continuous use. Research into the collection is a continuing process and a huge number of enquiries into its various aspects are received every year. Visitors to the collection are always welcome and many return over and over again as their work takes them into new areas of study.

The Symington Collection continues to fascinate, inspire and stimulate a wide range of students, researchers, historians and designers and remains a tribute to the men and women who played their part in the company's story.

Philip Warren, Keeper of Cultural Life

In memory of
Christopher Page and Eileen Nicholson
who both cared for this collection.

A Family Firm, 1830-1910

"Surely mention must be made of the export department constantly grappling with the tariff regulations of practically every country in the world and interpreting to the designing staff the widely divergent needs of women varying in build and differing in their views of the latest fashion. The narrow-waisted women from Malaya must have different models from those sent to fashion-conscious Iceland. Enigmatically, the suspenders on corsets for Manuchuria must be inches longer than standard: while corsets bound for Colombia, deep in South America, must be contained in parcels doubly wrapped and lashed for their journey by mule pack across the mountains."

These words come from the book 'In Our Own Fashion' which R. & W.H. Symington & Co. published in 1956. It sums up the extent to which the company's business had developed and prospered from modest beginnings in the High Street in Market Harborough over a hundred years before.

Market Harborough lies in the south-eastern corner of Leicestershire on the border with Northamptonshire, at the heart of the farmlands of the East Midlands. In the middle of the nineteenth century it was a prosperous market town on the road from Leicester to London, surrounded by large farms and estates. The surrounding area was famous for hunting and its local landed gentry, wealthy farmers, merchants and traders made it an attractive place for any young entrepreneur to set up a small business supplying them with goods and services.

In 1827 William Symington had left his family home in Lanarkshire and eventually settled in Market Harborough where he began a small but very successful tea, coffee and grocery warehouse and shop.

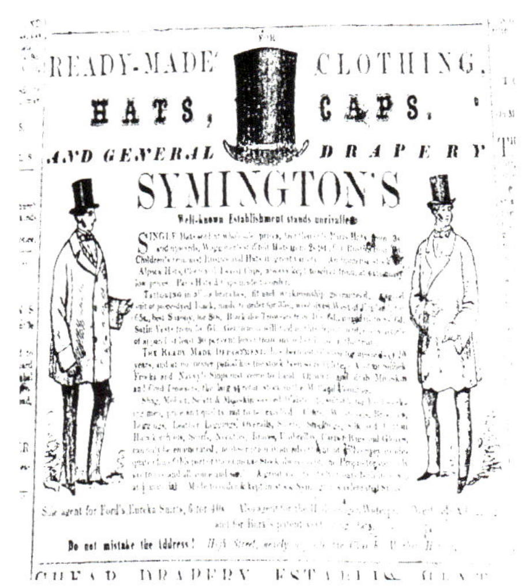

Press advertisement for James Symington's shop on the High Street, c1845.

Around 1830 James Symington, then aged nineteen, followed in his brother's footsteps and left Scotland for Leicestershire. He began a small business as a tailor, hatter and woollen draper and opened a shop next door to William's.

In 1832 William purchased some land in Little Bowden to the south of the town where he built a small food factory and moved from the shop next to James'. The old shop premises did not remain empty for long. Lured by the potential of a fashionable, discerning and prosperous female population in Market Harborough, Mrs Gold, a stay-maker from Warwick moved to the town with her daughter Sarah.

No doubt being neighbours and both involved in the business of selling the trappings of fashion to Market Harborough's wealthy women, James and Sarah would have had much to do with each other and, sometime around 1835, they married.

James and Sarah Symington photographed in the late 1850s.

Sarah's skills as a seamstress and stay maker were added to the Symington business and in 1850 James leased a small cottage in a yard at the rear of the High Street and here Sarah set up her workshop. The Symingtons employed three young assistants to make corsets for the wealthy women of the area. The business grew and James leased new, smarter premises on the High Street, which were soon refurbished; a bill-head dated 1862 shows the store with elegant columns and large showroom windows. By now James had included stay making in the description of his business and with his new wife he joined the ranks of the town's prosperous mercantile class.

Mr G Holt Harboro Sep 3 1862

LINEN & Woollen Draper HATTER

HOSIER and Stay MANUFACTURER.

Bot of James Symington

A Bill Head from 1862, depicting the Symington shop front in the High Street.

Sarah bore ten children, the eldest was Robert who, in 1855, at the age of eighteen travelled to America in search of business opportunities. What he found was a sewing machine that had been patented by Isaac Merrit Singer in 1851. (Machines that could stitch were not a new invention and they had been used in the manufacture of corsetry in the 1840s. Singer's patent protected the machine from any rivals and allowed him to develop the technology and so make a reliable lock stitch sewing machine.)

Detail from a print of a sewing factory from the middle of the 1850s showing women standing at their sewing machines.

Singer's machine was fixed to a large wooden box that also served as its packing crate. The operator stood at the machine and powered it by pushing a treadle with her foot.

The early introduction of the sewing machine into the Symington workshop undoubtedly aided production and saved much of the hard work of sewing tough fabrics by hand. There was, however, some reservation from the women who worked in the business. At the time mechanisation was still viewed with some apprehension and many that worked in traditional hand crafting industries feared for their livelihoods as machines were introduced into more and more areas of manufacturing. Eventually the staff were persuaded of the benefits of the new machines and the sewing of corsets at Symington's became, at least in part, mechanised.

As Sarah grew older her eyesight began to fail and she retired from the stay making business. Her skills had been in the production of fine corsetry, made to measure for a small and local clientele. Production was about to change completely and machines would revolutionise the corsetry industry, not just at Symington. What was required of the head of a concern like Symington's was a vision of the possibilities of mechanisation and the flair for business to implement it, not the training and skills of a traditional artisan worker. Control of the corsetry making business passed to Robert and his younger brother William Henry.

Robert Symington photographed in the early 1860s.

In 1861 Robert and William Henry took over part of a disused carpet factory in Adam and Eve Street in the middle of Market Harborough. Using modern production methods the company supplied some of the leading wholesalers in the country, producing corsets under their own name as well as those of their major clients.

The business continued to develop, steam power replaced the laborious foot treadles, more machines were brought into the factory, costs of production fell and orders increased. More staff were employed and Robert and William Henry brought their young sister Perry Gold into the business to look after the female workers. In 1876 the brothers managed to raise enough money to buy all of the factory building.

In 1880 the Midlands Times reported that R. & W.H. Symington were employing "some 1600 people and have about 500 machines running". Five hundred of these workers were employed at the Harborough factory with smaller branch factories in Leicester, Desborough, Welford and Rothwell and a host of outworkers who collected corsets from the factory to be finished at home In 1881 the business began to export its corsets to Australia and later to markets in Africa, Canada and the United States.

By the middle of the 1880s it was obvious that the business needed new capital in order for it to expand and develop. The Symington brothers were introduced to George Katz Warren who agreed to become a partner in the business and brought with him an injection of capital funding which, in 1884, allowed a new factory to be built in Church Gate, over the road from the existing factory.

By 1890 there were further factories in Manchester, Rugby and Farnham.

In 1892 Robert died, leaving William Henry and George Katz Warren in charge of the business.

In 1898 Katz Warren died and his share in the business was repaid in cash to his estate. The only way for the business to survive financially was for it to become a public company and on the 29th September 1898 R. & W.H. Symington & Co., Ltd. came into being. The family still controlled the running of the firm and the first directors were the three Symington brothers William Henry, Edward and James, Robert Howett who was Edward's brother in law and George Wilson Wilson who was one of the firm's agents.

The capital raised from the sale of shares amounted to £130,000, expansion followed almost immediately and in 1901 two new workrooms were added to the Church Gate Factory.

In 1905 Symington's lead in the home markets was being threatened by increased production from German corsetry manufacturers who had always been important manufacturers of mass-produced corsets. Frederick Cox, who had been elected to the board in 1903, was sent to Germany where he took advantage of the free trade conditions and bought cloth, which was for sale at greatly reduced prices. He returned to Britain with the cloth and, at Symington's Peterborough factory, made corsets of German design, in German fabric. They were cheaper than the German imports and the competition from Europe soon dissipated.

By the outbreak of the First World War in 1914 Symington was an international concern with the reputation of a market leader. The company was financially secure and was producing corsets and foundation garments that were well designed and made, and were reasonably priced. The company's marketing and advertising department was a leader in its field and it seemed that the new century would be one of opportunity for the business. In its hometown the Symington Company was the largest single employer in the town and literally dominated the lives of most of its inhabitants. The factory buildings towered over the centre of the Market Square and were a clear landmark on the main road from London.

William Henry Symington photographed in the middle of the1890s.

A Family Affair

"We started there for nothing... we came and sat with our mothers, and we learned things from them."

Mrs Hancock, who worked in the French Room and the Liberty Bodice room from 1922, speaking in 1981.

Late nineteenth century factory based mass production was always hard work, the working day was often long and tiring, tasks were repetitive and wages were seldom high. Some employers, including R. & W.H. Symington did provide their workforces with benefits and working conditions that were better than the norm.

R. & W.H. Symington was for many years the largest employer in Market Harborough, and the company and the family who controlled it had a great impact on the town and its people.
The factory buildings were, for their time, light and clean, although former workers remember them as being noisy. There was good sanitary provision and there were drinking fountains for the workers on each floor. The working day began at 6am; there was a break for breakfast and one at mid-day.
The working week ended at 1pm on Saturday.
Late shifts were often worked when urgent orders or deliveries were required and in the summer months it was not unusual for the Symington workers still to be at the factory until 10pm.

Sewing Room workers, c1890.

From the very beginning the company provided social and recreational activity for its workforce. On January 22nd 1881 the Midlands Times reported that "On Monday last, Messrs W.H. and R. Symington & Co., gave about 230 of their employees an afternoon on the ice.
Taking advantage of the frost the firm engaged a special train to convey the party to a piece of water known as the Welham ballast Hole, some 3 miles from Market Harborough." The report continues with scenes of dancing and skating on the ice to the sound of the factory brass band (which had been formed in 1870). On the return to Harborough "the proceedings were continued by a Ball in the Corn Exchange". There were further outings to the seaside and the 'regatta' on the canal at Market Harborough.

Perry Gold Symington, photographed around 1900.

Many of the facilities and social benefits that the workers enjoyed were due to the efforts of Perry Gold Symington, the younger sister of Robert and William Henry. The brothers had taken Perry Gold into the business to look after the welfare of the female workers and each one that came to work at the factory was interviewed by her. She was acutely aware of the social and employment issues that affected many young women at the turn of the twentieth century. She herself became a board director in 1911 but only after nearly thirty years of tireless work for the family firm. Women's welfare was Perry Gold Symington's principal concern, she began a social club for female employees and in 1920 converted 'The Elms', her late brother's home, into a hostel for orphan girls.

Miss Symington was also responsible for the conduct of the female workers and would patrol the different departments at the factory. Cissy Abbott who worked at Symington from 1918 remembers her "coming round like a ship in full sail... she swept through the rooms. If you did anything outside the factory that wasn't just right and (she) got to know, the next day she'd have you... on the carpet."

Perhaps her lasting legacy to the company was the building of the clubroom in the 1901 extension to the factory. The Symington clubroom was the hub of social life at the factory. Here plays were performed, concerts given and every Saturday night there was a dance. Miss Symington would make her entrance to the clubroom surrounded by her assistants and only then could the dancing begin. She sat on a small stage and ensured that the young couples behaved with propriety. Cissy Abbott attended many clubroom dances and saw Miss Symington controlling their behaviour. "When they were doing the Lancers, if they lifted them off their feet she'd send one of the forewomen down the room to tell them about it... She'd go 'No, no' as you passed the stage and were being flung around."

In 1919 the Symington board purchased land near the factory and built a sports ground for the staff. The workers at Market Harborough had always been interested in sport and football was a great favourite. There were football teams from different departments of the factory and the Saturday afternoon Harborough League featured many from the company. The Symington sports ground was officially opened in 1921 and a bowls pavilion added some years later.

The French Room football team, 1914.

"It was a thing to be at Symington's. I'm not saying they paid well, but it was the thing to be there. Let's face it... Symington's recreation ground was the finest... in this country, cricket, bowls, tennis."

Mr K. Gilbert, who worked in the cutting room during the 1930s.

By the early 1920s the Symington factory had its own library, clinic and canteen and female workers had their own rest room.

The women's rest room, 1929.

Facilities such as these made the reputation of the company as an employer a good one (despite their famously low pay). From most accounts the factory was a strong community in which people were generally happy to help their colleagues. "Any bad work you put right in your own time... what used to happen, if you were pally with the girls around you, they all used to do a bit for you... help each other out." (Cissy Abbott)

The factory staff always came together to celebrate major local and national events. Coronations, jubilees and wartime victories were all cause for celebration and the factory buildings were trimmed up with bunting, streamers and flags. Annual local events such as the Harborough Carnival were an opportunity for elaborate floats and parades in which the Symington workers took an active part.

In 1956, the company celebrated its centenary with great flair, decorating the factory, holding shows of their corsetry collection and publishing a book entitled 'In Our Own Fashion', which recorded the achievements of the Symington company and the individual members of the family.

In 1967 the Courtaulds Group took over the factory and the family's influence over the company diminished. In 1980 the offices and some of the workrooms were sold to the Harborough District Council to be turned into premises for offices, a museum and a library. The factory continued to make underwear and swimwear until May 1990, when production finally stopped and the factory closed with the final loss of 150 jobs.

"In Symington's, probably your grandmother had been there, your aunts had been there, so you went there, that's how it was, a proper family affair."

Miss Cissy Abbott, who worked at Symington from 1918-1968, speaking in 1983.

A sewing Room decorated for the Coronation of King George VI, 1937.

Mid Victorian Fashion 1860-1880

Fashion Plate from the magazine 'Le Monde Elegant', May 1878.

The ideal of a fashionable woman changed during the twenty years between 1860 and 1880. At the beginning of the 1860s those women who had the time and money to enjoy fashionable clothes presented a silhouette that resembled a graceful bell, with large encompassing skirts and a tightly fitted bodice. The bodice was relatively short and cut square at the waist. The waist was made to appear even smaller than it was by the fullness of the skirt, which was gathered into the waistband.

Beneath these outer garments, and nestling amidst layers of cotton and silk underclothes was a corset, which gave shape to the body, controlled and supported the bust and corrected the wearer's posture. The corset was an essential garment in a woman's wardrobe and it would have been unthinkable for any respectable woman not to wear one. A typical corset of the mid 1860s would have fitted across the bust with boning to push the breasts slightly upwards. Boned, quilted or corded panels in the corset controlled the waist and stomach and the hip sections flared gently out from the waist producing a graceful hourglass shape.

In the early 1860s the French invention of a busk fastening which allowed the wearer to put a corset on unaided revolutionised corsets forever. The metal busk closed the centre front of the corset with a series of metal loops which hooked onto studs. The flat metal strips from which the loops and studs projected gave the front of the corset rigidity and supported the front of the wearer's torso, balancing the support from the central lacing at the back. Together these two central areas imposed a strict upright posture that made bending at the waist difficult and uncomfortable.

During the 1870s a style of dress that was cut without a seam at the waist was introduced by the couturier Charles Frederick Worth. It was called the 'princess line' and the effect was instantly to lengthen the appearance of a woman's torso. The dresses fitted like a glove and the bodices, which were often boned themselves, were extremely tight. The wearer required a corset that defined her bust, lengthened and reduced her waist and controlled her hips far more than previously. Outer garments were elaborately trimmed and decorated often with machine-made lace and embroidery. Corsets were often similarly decorative with deep bands of ribbon-trimmed lace, and embroidery on the casings that held the boning.

Fashions and the technologies that help to create them come and go. Production techniques that are discarded in one period are, very often, re-discovered and reintroduced in another. At the beginning of the 1870s corsets usually relied on their cut, stiff fabric, boning and quilting to control and give shape to the wearer's figure. By the end of the decade a more gently curved and smoother line was dictated by outer fashions and the corset manufacturers reintroduced the cording process which had been used at the beginning of the century. Cording gave supple support, was flexible and produced a smooth silhouette that was flattering beneath a tight bodice.

As the 1870s progressed outer fashions became narrower and tighter, with skirts that draped into a bustle at the small of the back. The bodices of dresses began to get shorter as the bustle became more and more pronounced and by the end of the decade a very different silhouette had appeared.

During the late 1870s newly developed embroidery and flossing machines began to take over the decorative work that had previously been done by hand. This sample of embroidery shows the quality of work that could be achieved even when stitching across boning and through three layers of heavy fabric.

c1860.

Closed front corset of red (now faded to pale orange) and black cotton lasting. The corset is stiffened down the centre front with a wooden busk. Corsets of this type were fitted and closed by lacing down the centre back and any minor changes to the fit could be achieved by adjusting the laces. It was impossible for such a corset to be put on by the wearer without help from either a member of their family or a household servant.

Museum ref. A2

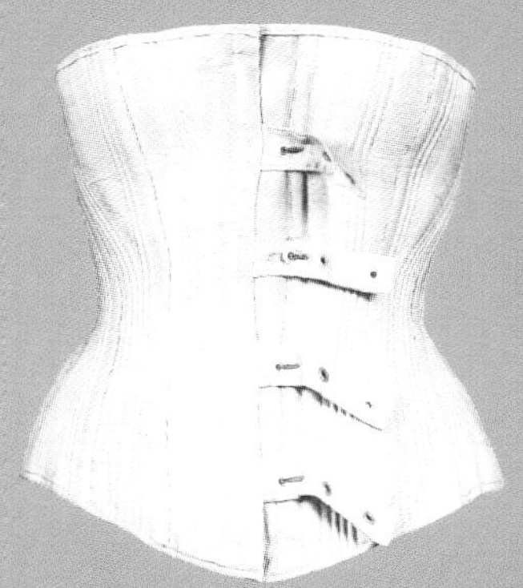

c1870-1875.

This unusual corset has no lacing at the back, the fit could be adjusted by using the straps at the front of the garment which have reinforced eyelets and metal hooks. The support is made from a combination of split cane and cotton cording. The combined fastening and adjusting device at the front of the corset is unique in the collection but must have proved bulky and unsightly beneath the close fitting bodices of the 1870s.

Museum ref. A4

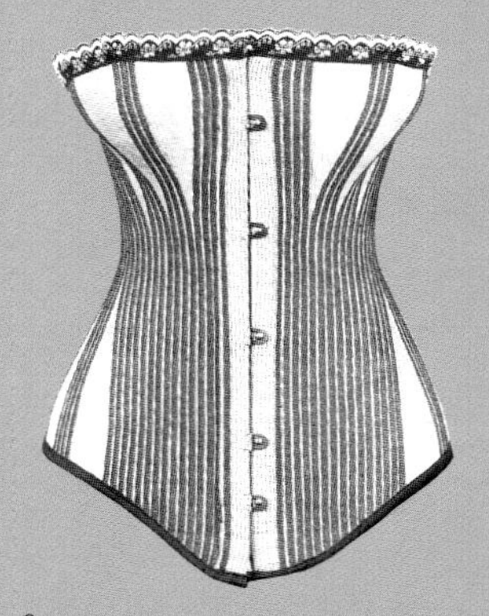

c1875.

This corset, in shades of indigo cotton, is made on a corset loom, each half being woven in one piece without the need for pattern cutting and complicated sewing. Hemp twine is hand threaded through each row of mock saddle stitching to give further support and the finished garment is much more flexible and comfortable than traditionally produced corsets of the same period.

Museum ref. A10

c1875.

By the mid 1860s front busk fastenings were in general use in British corsets. The four studs and clasps down the front of the busk allowed the wearer to put the corset on themselves: a small revolution in clothing technology that allowed fashionable women to dress themselves without aid. This corset is made from black cotton lasting and uses a combination of machine stitched cording and quilting to give support and to control the figure. The stitching and flossing is worked in amber thread giving a distinctive and decorative finish to the garment.

Museum ref. A5

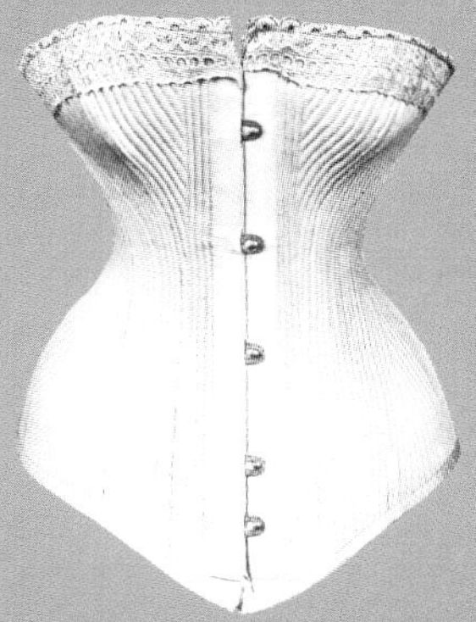

c1880.

This corset, made from khaki coutil, is stiffened using the process of cotton cording. The pattern pieces are precisely cut and the cording process gives shape, support and a gentle series of curves to the corset. The cording process meant that corsets could be produced without using whalebone or cane boning.

Museum ref. A7

The Original Guaranteed Corset

Guaranteed to wear 12 Months.

And the Makers undertake to make good any defect which may occur during that time.

EXCELLENT IN

Style,

Shape,

AND

Finish;

Possessing all the elements for

Strength and Comfort.

"This enterprising firm has lately introduced another novelty, which we feel sure will be highly appreciated by the thrifty, viz: a Corset guaranteed to wear 12 months. This is an entirely new departure in the right direction. We cannot too highly recommend it."—"Invention."

"These Corsets are worth every penny of their price without the additional and great advantage of being guaranteed to wear for 12 months."—"Trade Journal."

The world-wide reputation our Guaranteed Corset has earned during upwards of TWENTY YEARS, has tempted rival makers to imitate it in inferior materials, without, however, warranting the very parts which usually give way first, such as busks, &c., &c., We would therefore remind the public that our system is to Guarantee absolutely every part of our Corset for 12 months, without any reservation.

When purchasing, please see that the lining is stamped as follows, which is the Trade Mark of the originators of the system of Guaranteeing Corsets for 12 months.

ORIGINAL MAKE.

Trade advertisement for the *'Original Guaranteed Corset'* which features the R. & W.H. Symington brand in the bottom right hand corner. This brand mark sometimes appears stamped in the inside of a corset.

Late Victorian Fashion

1880-1900

c1890.

Printed box top from *'The Surprise Corset'* one of the many named corsets that Symington put out into the market. Very often these corsets were a standard model that appeared with a new name and new packaging.

Theatre dresses from Le Salon de la mode, 1887.

At the beginning of the 1880s the fashionable woman was wearing a complicated and elaborate confection of rich, heavy fabrics ornamented and decorated with trimmings of beads, fringing, tassels and lace. The bustle was, by now, an exaggerated and high drape of knotted and puffed fabric that seemed to grow out of a slim skirt, the hem of which still hovered just above the ground. The 'Princess' line was still a popular construction technique for bodices, which became shorter to take account of the high bustle at the back. Fashion plates of the period show an idealised view of women's figures, which had sloping, narrow shoulders, a generous curved bust and a long, narrow V shaped torso.

The corset was still an imperative part of a woman's wardrobe and became increasingly constricting around the waist. In the 1860s a waistline might appear smaller in contrast to the spreading skirts of a dress, but by the 1880s the visual difference was not so acute so corsets were more heavily boned and laced more tightly at the back.

There has been much discussion, both at the time and in subsequent years, about the tight lacing of corsets. Much of the debate has centred on the publication of correspondence in 1867 in 'The Englishwoman's Domestic Magazine' which argued the benefits of tight lacing especially for young girls. Many of the correspondents were men with a sexual interest in tight lacing and the subject should be treated with some scepticism. There were undoubtedly those women who engaged in tight lacing as a matter of personal preference. Then, as now there were prominent celebrities and socialites who raised their profiles by emphasising their own extremely slim figures.

Some members of the health professions protested about the practice of tight lacing, arguing that it was detrimental to the physical development of young women and distorted the internal organs. Throughout the 1880s dress reformers and members of the aesthetic movement argued for more freedom in women's dress and designed their own, loosely draped garments which were heavily influenced by their idealised view of medieval clothes. Even many of these clothes, which were worn by a tiny fraction of the population, would have been worn with a corset but the lack of emphasis on the waist meant that it need not be tightly laced.

Mainstream fashion continued to focus its attention on the waist. By the beginning of the 1890s the bustle skirt had disappeared and bodices became longer and more constricting around the ribcage. These dress bodices were themselves boned to give extra shape and support and, when worn with a corset, a bust bodice or bust improver gave a fashionable hourglass or 'wasp waisted' figure.

The corsets that helped to achieve the new figure were heavily boned and technically quite complicated to make. By the early 1890s new boning technology including the successful introduction of steel supports meant that corsets could control and support more powerfully than before. The end of the century saw some of the best-designed and manufactured corsets that came out of the Symington factory. New colours were introduced and the Symington machinists excelled in applying machine embroidery to the casings of the boning. Marketing and packaging design also flourished at the company with some of the most creative and decorative designs being made for the boxes in which the corsets were sold.

1890.

Corset box top from *'The Pretty Housemaid'*. This was sold as being the "strongest and cheapest corset ever made" and was fitted with a busk protector which stopped the busk front from breaking as the wearer stooped or bent over. What is fascinating about this corset and its marketing is that it was directly targeted at young women in domestic service, which was then the largest employment sector in Britain. It demonstrates that young, working class women were a recognised consumer group with a small disposable income and an interest in fashion.

Museum ref. B11

c1890.

Display card for the *'Morn and Noon'* corsets which were sold together in one box. This was more than a marketing or retail gimmick as fashionable women required different styles of corset for different purposes, occasions and even different times of the day.

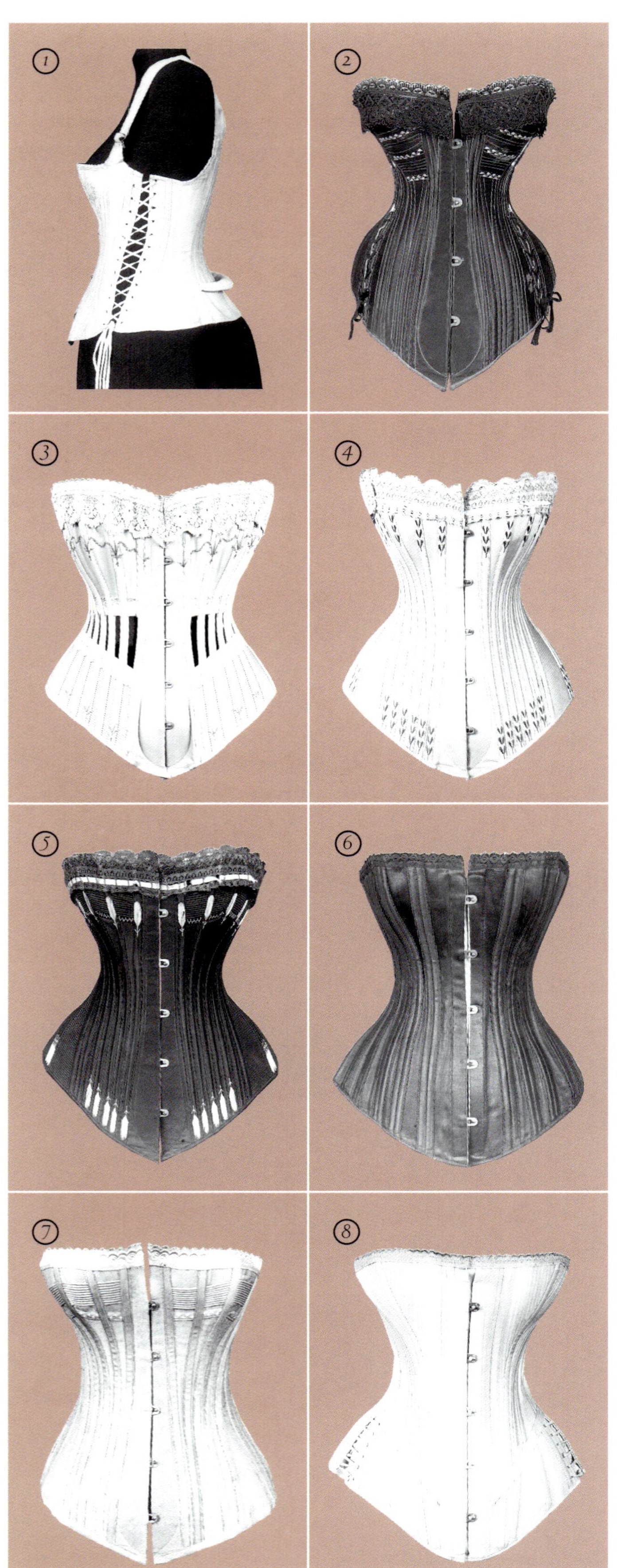

1. c1880.

'Queen Bess' corset, designed and made in the U.S.A. The corset has laces down both sides and is closed down the centre front with a busk which includes a patent busk protector that was supposed to prevent breaking as a result of wear. At the centre back is a crescent-shaped pad to support the fashionable bustle skirts of the 1880s.

Museum ref. A29

2. c1880.

Maternity corset of black sateen trimmed with lace and decorative machine stitching at the bust. Even during pregnancy Victorian women were expected to make some attempt to achieve a fashionable figure. Laces at the sides of the abdomen allowed for some adjustment to the corset but it is still fully boned (40 strips of whalebone) and has a heavy steel busk down the centre front.

Museum ref. A37

3. c1895.

Ventilated corset for 'coolness during wear in tropical zones'. As Britain's Empire grew, more and more women travelled to and lived in the colonies. Faced with a tropical climate but still insistent on presenting the ideal image of a fashionable European lady, women required corsets which allowed a modicum of comfort in the heat. There are 22 supports in the corset, but lightweight cane is used in the place of whalebone.

Museum ref. B8

4. c1890.

A wasp waist corset made from khaki coutil with decorative flossing and feather stitching in dark brown and cream. Strips of whalebone create a gently flaring bust and narrow waist and meet together over the abdomen to flatten and control the stomach. The side panels are created with vertical and diagonal string cording.

Museum ref. B16

5. c1890.

Wasp-waist corset of black cotton lasting decorated with gold feather stitching and gold ribbon slotted through a lace trim at the bust. The accentuated waist is created using a combination of vertical boning and horizontal and diagonal cording at the bust and hips. Such garments combine seductive design and decoration with technically brilliant cut and manufacture.

Museum ref. B30

6. 1895.

Black sateen corset made in the U.S.A. In 1885 a patent was issued for the pre-curved flat steel strips of which 40 are used to support this garment. The pre-formed steels are so rigid that this corset can stand up without support and retains its shape perfectly.

Museum ref. B32a

7. c1895.

Corset with a novel corded and flared bust section that gave an exaggerated line to the bust that was so unusual that it carried a patent. Stamped on the inside of the corset is its remarkably cheap original retail price of 1s.11d.

Museum ref. B59

8. 1898.

Maternity corset made in Canada (patented 1896). The use of elastic in the abdominal laces meant that the corset would adjust to the body's shape during the development of a pregnancy. The elastic would give subtle changes during a day's wear and could be re-laced to allow for more freedom as the pregnancy went on.

Museum ref. B48

CAVÉ'S PATENT.

Strongly recommended by the Medical Profession.

Extract from "The Lancet."

"The Corsets of Madame Cavé are the best we have ever seen, and will give perfect support. Ladies inclined to embonpoint may derive benefit from them, the belt keeping the figure down to its proper proportion, at the same time ensuring great comfort, as it cannot, by any chance slip out of its place, as so many belts do, causing great inconvenience and sometimes pain."

May be had of all respectable Drapers, or by letter, of

MADAME CAVE,

HARRIS'S, 159, PICCADILLY, LONDON.

White, 10s. 6d., 15s. 6d., 21s., 31s. 6d.; Black or Scarlet, 12s. 9d., 18s. 6d., 25s.; White for Nursing, 17s. 9d.; Black Satin, 42s. The Belt only, best quality, White, 9s. 3d.; Black, 10s. 6d.

This 1880s advertisement for Madame Cavé's patent belt corset features recommendations from 'The Lancet', the journal of the medical profession.

It may be that this advertisement was aimed at pregnant women as well as those suffering from 'embonpoint' at a time when such delicate matters as pregnancy were not openly mentioned in advertisements.

1884.

Madame Cavé's patent corset with buckle fastening over belt. This corset is supported by 64 whalebone strips and has an over belt which controls a front stomach section attached by six buckles.

Museum ref. A26

THE GREATEST NOVELTIES IN CORSETS FOR THIS SEASON ARE
SYMINGTON'S EYELETTED SEAM ✠ AND ✠ SYMINGTON'S DIVIDED BUSK,

Eyeletted from top to bottom of each seam, making the strongest seam ever known, and providing the necessary ventilation, without which no article of clothing is perfect. The makers undertake to replace, gratis, every pair giving way at the seams.

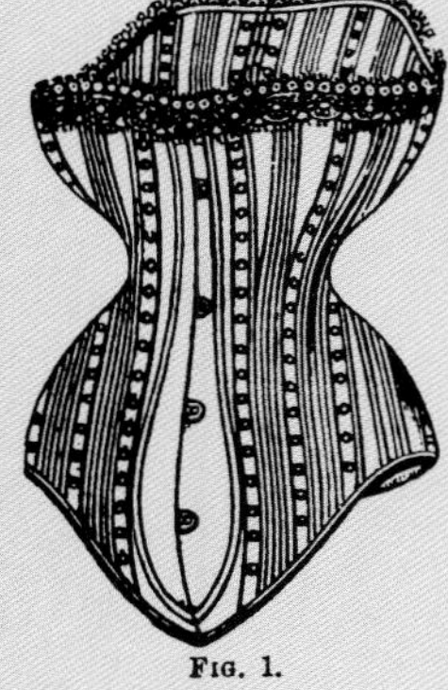

Fig. 1.

Drab, Fawn, White, 47s. 6d. per doz.

Black, Cardinal, 63s. per doz.

NOW EXHIBITING

AT THE

INTERNATIONAL CRYSTAL PALACE

AND

HEALTH EXHIBITIONS,

LONDON,

And for which a Silver Medal has been awarded.

FROM WHOLESALE HOUSES.

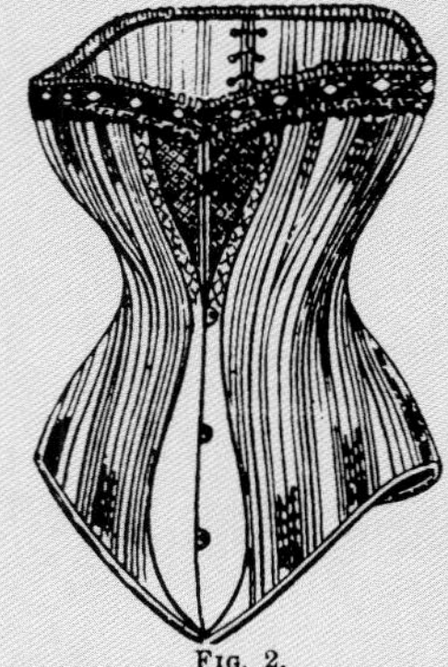

Fig. 2.

Removes the gravest objection to the ordinary Corset, namely, the usual injurious pressure upon the delicate and vital organs of the chest, and meets the present demand for hygienic dress reform. The upper portions of the busk are curved outwards, leaving the organs of respiration entirely free, and, being ground down to the finest consistency, form beautifully yielding supports to the bosom part of the corset. This invention has been elaborated from the suggestions of an eminent medical man, who writes the Patentees as follows: "I am more than pleased with your invention, which I consider perfection. It will, I feel sure, entirely remove the distressing conditions which I have described. You may rely upon my influence in recommending the article to my numerous patients, and I trust your meritorious efforts will be fully appreciated by a grateful public." Manufactured of the best material only. In a variety of colours, **63s.** to **95s.** per doz.

A trade advertisement for Symington's Patented Eyletted Seam and Divided Busk corsets, which were part of the company's stand at the Crystal Palace in 1884. The corsets were sold on the basis of being health-giving and were a response to the growing demands of health and dress reform. It is interesting to note the difference in the trade price for a dozen corsets between 'standard' corset colours and black and cardinal red ones.

Museum ref. A13 for the Eyeletted corset.

c1895.

Printed box tops for wasp-waist corsets of the middle of the 1890s. Symington had their own design and printing departments and this period produced some of its most decorative packaging. The packaging incorporated some of the major design trends of the period including the Art Nouveau style shown on the right.

Bodices, Bust Improvers & Brassières

1890.
The *'Khiva Corset'* (Reg. Patent no. 15149) was made to fasten over a specially designed waist and hip girdle and was designed to support and control the bust. It is made of black sateen, trimmed with black machine made lace and has triple rows of boning which run from the shoulder strap to the waist. The bodice closes with a strap, which is retained with a metal buckle.

Museum ref. B40

c1890.
The *'Lemon Cup'* bust improver. From the outside this garment resembles two circular pads contained within a simple white cotton pouch. Inside, the pads reveal that they contain a light, coiled spring packed into a pad of bleached horsehair. The springs are anchored onto strips of whalebone that run horizontally. When the garment was pinned over a corset, or into a shift or camisole, the breasts would push the whalebone into a deep outward curve and force the spring out into the pad to give the impression of a larger, more generous bust.

Museum ref. B200

c1895.
Frilled bust improver attached to a deep bust bodice (illustrated inside out). The frills could be adjusted by tie-tapes to give different amounts of fullness to the bust. These were worn inside the bodice leaving a smooth, pleated front. The shoulder straps and neck of the bodice are trimmed with a fine machine-made lace.

Museum ref. B202

Over the last one hundred years the ideal shape, size and position of women's breasts has changed far more frequently and more drastically than at any other time in fashion history. Corsets, bust improvers and later bras all played their part in defining, changing and sometimes even creating the line of the breasts.

The bust section of a corset controls the breasts in two ways, by supporting and slightly lifting them and by dividing them with the top of the busk. Different shapes, depths and styles of corset control and support the bust in different ways. A corset cannot significantly alter the shape or size of the bust, but it can position the breasts differently, giving the effect of a higher or lower bust. Until the late nineteenth century a woman who wished to have a differently shaped bust line had to resort to padding, either her corset, or the lining of her bodice.

During the 1860s the fashion for a high bust line was achieved by inserting small pads of wool into the bodice lining. When worn over the natural bust the padded bodice gave a gently rounded shape to the breasts.

By the 1890s the fashion for a much more generous and overtly curved bust was well established. Women began to wear new undergarments that helped them to achieve the fashionable shape with its distinctive 'pouter pigeon' chest. 'Bust improvers' or bust bodices were garments that were worn over the top of the corset and inside the bodice of the dress. They were varied in their construction and used everything from frills of cotton to strips of whalebone and even springs to create the ideal of the fashionable bust with its single, deep, overhanging curve. This was the first time that a separate garment had been used to alter the shape, size or position of a woman's bust.

Different manufacturers, retailers, women's magazines and customers used different names for the many types of bust improver that were available on the market. Advertisements tended to refer to the garments by the French term 'brassières' and by the outbreak of World War One the term was almost universal.

The brassière, became a vital part of a woman's wardrobe and over the next fifty years it was designed and made in a myriad of styles and types, which created new bust lines every time that fashion dictated a new change.

Early brassières bear little resemblance to the modern day bra, they resemble white cotton camisoles but have support, shaping and are more robust.

The earliest brassière in the collection that shares anything in common with contemporary bra design dates from 1915. This brassière is made from soft cotton tricot, has adjustable shoulder straps and a bust panel that is divided into cups, so separating the breasts. Based on the design by the American Caresse Crosby(Mary Phelps Jacob) this simple garment may be one of her own commercially produced garments. Crosby claimed to be the inventor of the bra and told the story of how she had instructed her lady's maid to sew together two silk handkerchiefs and fix them onto some ribbon shoulder straps. The bra, with separate supporting cups, was born although it took nearly twenty years for it to become an acceptable, popular garment.

At the same time that Crosby was developing her new design the Parisian sultan of the fashion world, Paul Poiret was claiming to have liberated women from the corset. His long, slim dresses were based, in part, on the early nineteenth century fashion for a high waist and a high, rounded bust. Poiret was a great champion of the brassière, and advocated its use with his designs.

After World War One, the opulent curves of the late Edwardian period were finally lost and young women affected a boyish slimness that called for no bust at all. Deep, flattening 'bust bandeaux' were introduced, these used improved rubber and elastic technology to give stretch and comfort whilst flattening the bust. The bandeaux were made from elasticated knitted and lace fabrics and simply pulled down over the wearer's head or had simple side closures.

If the 1920s bust bandeaux were about not having a bust at all, then the new brassières of the early 1930s were about giving shape, support and definition to a natural bust line which showed through the clinging bias-cut garments of the day.

The brassière, was now firmly established and was made in a wide variety of styles for every different figure type. By 1940 Symington's yearly collections usually included over fifty different brassière styles.

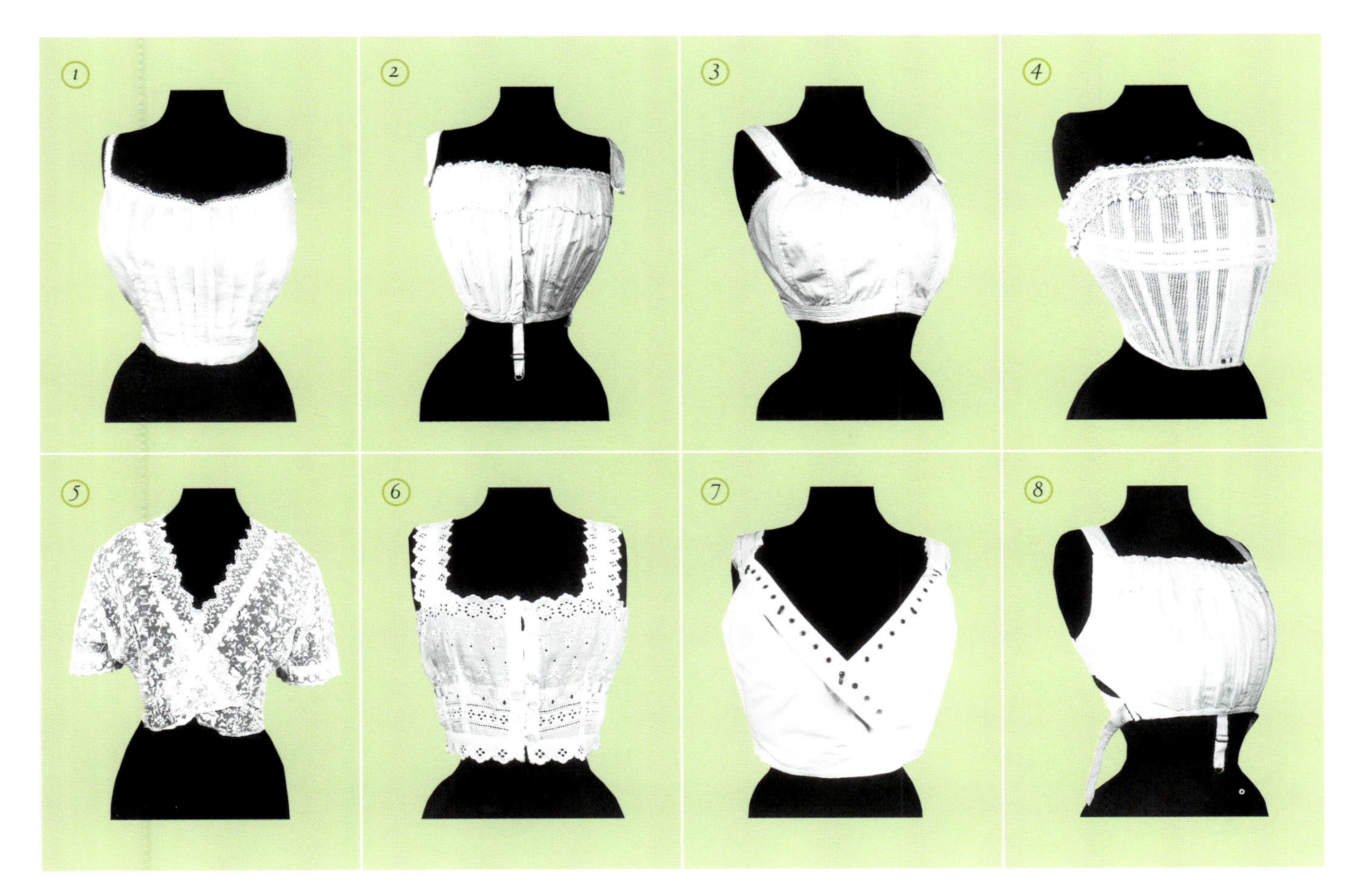

1. c1895.

Deep bust bodice in fine cotton cambric with a tucked front which is frilled on the inside.

Museum ref. B207

2. c1900.

Bust bodice with a button front fastening and back lacing, adjustable shoulder straps and lace and ribbon trim. Detachable whaleboning inside the front of the bodice is joined with tie cords to adjust the fullness of the curve of the bust.
The strap at the bottom of the centre front has a metal loop for anchoring the bust bodice to the hooks of a corset.

Museum ref. B201

3. c1900.

Button front bust bodice with back lacing and adjustable shoulder straps. The hem and bust panels contain layers of machine cording to support, shape and control the bust.

Museum ref. B204

4. 1902.

Deep supporting bust bodice or bust improver in heavily starched strong cotton net with deep horizontal and vertical boning. The curved front is kept in place by triple layers of boning of goose quills, which have been bound together by hand with cotton thread.

Museum ref. C200

5. c1905.

Camisole made from a width of Leavers scalloped-edge lace. Ribbon is slotted down the front and around the cuffs of the sleeves. There is a short, concealed back lacing panel and a waist cord to anchor the camisole into place.

Museum ref. C208

6. c1905.

Short camisole-style bodice in Broderie Anglaise.
The front closes with button fastenings and the fit is adjusted with back lacing. There are four strips of lightweight boning beneath the bust.

Museum ref. C209

7. c1905.

Back supporting bodice designed to alleviate upper back pain and shoulder stooping. There are 48 flat steels for support and the bodice would have been worn over another, conventional corset.

Museum ref. C210

8. c1910.

Bust improver with patent crossover back support. Inside the front are ten removable whalebone strips with four adjustable slide tapes, these could be adjusted to give a more or less pronounced curve to the bust as desired.

Museum ref. C204

c1910.

Button front bust bodice. A further step towards freedom of movement were the insets of suspender elastic which are set into the shoulder straps and along each side panel of the garment. There are ten strips of curved whalebone inside the front of the bust section and more strips of flat boning down the back.

Museum ref. C206

1911.

The *'Reform Dress'* bodice, patented in 1911, was designed to be worn over the top of a low fitting corset to control the diaphragm. The bust sections are made from cotton net with a broad central panel, which fastens with buttons. The shoulder straps are adjustable and cross over at the back. Two sections control the area beneath the bust and the waist and these can be tightened using sliding buckles at the back. The points at the bottom of the bodice have buttons so that drawers could be attached.

Museum ref. D202

c1915.

Bust bodice made from forty graded sections of Barmen edging, stitched in a gentle crescent to vertical strips of embroidered cotton. The whole is anchored at the waist with a ribbon drawstring. The bodice closes with a button fastening and 5cm frilled elastic is inserted at both side seams for comfort.

Museum ref. D206

1915.

Brief brassière in soft cotton tricot based on Caresse Crosby's original patented design (this may be one of her own commercial products). This brassière was completely revolutionary and it was over twenty years before such styles were generally accepted.

Museum ref. D200

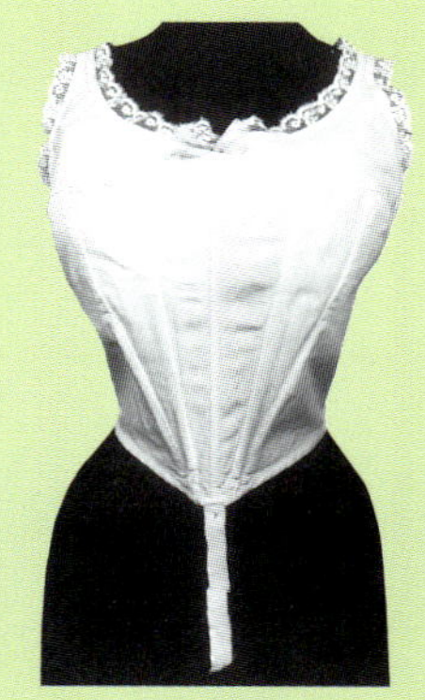

1915.

This American deep fitting, lightly boned bodice is important, not for its styling, which is fairly common, but for the fact that stamped on its original label is the name *'DeBeboise Brassière'*. This is an early reference to the garment that would later become familiar to us all as the 'bra'. Also printed on the label is the bust size in inches, an early use of accurate sizing in foundation garments.

Museum ref. D203

1. c1920.

It was this form of flat-fronted bandeau that was to completely dominate the shape of the brassière throughout the 1920s. The boyish flat-chested look, which was fashionable amongst young women, called for special garments that flattened rather than accentuated the breasts. Elastics and lace were both used to create broad panels to wrap around the bust. For those women who didn't want to invest in a commercial bandeau, a silk stocking tied around the breasts would suffice.

Museum ref. D201

2. 1921.

Patent bust improver of white cotton cambric with front button fastening and back lacing. The patent involves the crossed bust straps with an uplift diaphragm piece in double cotton drill and plain elastic.

Museum ref. E200

3. 1925.

A slip on bandeau in cream elasticated Cluny lace. The lace was called ventilated elastic and was supplied to R. & W.H. Symington by Clutsom and Kemp Ltd. The bandeau flattened the bust and was very easy to put on; making it ideally suited to both the fashions and the lifestyles of the time.

Museum ref. E206

4. c1925.

Bust bodice with patent side lacing. The side lacing mechanism retained its popularity for over forty years and sales were such that a whole production unit at the factory was dedicated to its making.

Museum ref. E204

5. 1930.

Brief brassière in white crêpe satin, inset with fine net across each cup. The central panel is made from a decorative lace. The cups are more defined in this bra which closes with hooks and eyes at the back and has narrow adjustable shoulder straps.

Museum ref. E218

6. 1930.

Deep brassière of pink broche made by Warner's of the U.S.A. This brassière, with a straight front and side fastening has a diaphragm lining for extra support. The back is strengthened and supported with a deep panel of elastic.

Museum ref. E207

Corsets

1900-1915

c1910.
Printed corset box top showing an ideal of the long, gentle curves of the fashionable woman of the age.

CORSET

c1900.
Contrasting ecru and brown sateen straight front corset. Although it maintains the small waist (visually accentuated by its dramatic two-tone boning casings) this corset has a straight front rather than a curved busk, a feature that would predominate in later styles.

Museum ref. B13

The first fifteen years of the twentieth century, which we call Edwardian despite the death of King Edward VII in 1910, saw a radical change in the ideal shape of a fashionable woman. The wasp waist of the late 1890s would continue into the early 1900s but there was a gradual change in the emphasis of the silhouette. The fullness of the bust developed into a full pouter pigeon chest, overhanging a small waist that was, along with the hips and bottom, pushed backwards. The shape that this distortion made was referred to as the S bend, as a woman's figure resembled the curves of the letter S.

Dress bodices gradually developed greater fullness at the front, decorative ruffles and trimmings gave a generous curve to the bust, which was accentuated by the wearing of bust improvers beneath the outer garments. Skirts also had a new shape achieved by being cut with gored panels, which gave fullness at the hem and a smooth, close-fitting flatness over the hips, and into the waist.

Clothes for summer and winter, for daytime and evening, for town and for country were all very different. Many women adopted some elements of mannish tailoring for their day clothes but the contrast between daytime tailoring, which was rather severe and undecorated, and the luxury of diaphanous, fragile and very 'feminine' evening clothes, with their deep décolletage and elaborately embellished fabrics must have been startling.

Whether the clothes were for daytime or for evening they all required a corset that created a small waist, controlled the hips by pushing them backwards and, when worn with a bust improver, gave a pronounced elevated curve and fullness to the bust. The corsets had short, flat busks and fitted lower at the bust than before. Boning was still heavy but the main feature of change was the gradual increase in the depth of the skirt that stretched over the hips and across the bottom. By 1905 it was usual for corsets to have attached stocking suspenders.

Corset design began to reflect the design and decoration of lingerie, in which the finest silks, satins and cottons were used to create fluid, sensuous garments that were a mixture of underwear and the sort of garment that a woman might wear in the privacy of her bedroom or boudoir. The beautiful laces, ribbon and the pale pastel colours used in lingerie were adopted by the corsetry manufacturers who introduced new colours including pale pink and yellow, duck egg blue and eau de Nil.

In 1910 Symington introduced a corset which was actually snowy white (white shades had previously been off white,very light grey or pale cream). The white corsets were difficult to make without getting dirty. A special workroom was created in which the dirt could be controlled and the workers were issued with white overalls to prevent coloured lint from their clothing falling onto the corsets. The seamstresses dipped their hands into bowls of chalk so that they didn't leave dirty finger marks as they sewed. In 1913 Frederick Cox, the director responsible for marketing, introduced a new pale peach colour called 'blush white' based on the colour of a rose that he grew in his garden. Even more seductively the blush white corsets were packed into their boxes and sprayed with rose-scented perfume.

By 1908 the so-called Directoire style, created by Paul Poiret, gave women a new, slim, long and gently curved silhouette with a high waist reminiscent of the empire line of the early nineteenth century. Poiret claimed to have liberated women's waists from the corset, but although his designs did away with a tightly constricted waist they called for a long corset which stretched over the hips and down the thighs. Freeing the waist but shackling the legs was one of Poiret's legacies to the corsetry industry; the other was his championing of the brassière.

The corsets that fitted beneath the Directoire line fitted under the bust and used heavy flat boning to create a long tubular shape with a straight posture, the complete opposite of the previously fashionable S bend. The skirts of outer clothes were extremely narrow and restricted women from walking with anything more than shallow steps. The corsets similarly had long tight skirts reaching well down the thighs and made walking with long strides difficult and often painful.

The outbreak of World War One in 1914 had little immediate impact on fashion but as the war dragged on the social upheaval that it brought changed women's clothing forever.

c1900.

The *'Bird's Wing'* corset is made from 42 individually shaped cotton pieces and boned with the same number of whalebone strips. The intricate construction means that, when open, the corset forms the shape of a bird's wing.

Museum ref. B23

c1900.

Diagonal-seam corset in black sateen, designed to give a more pronounced figure line as well as adding strength to the corset. The boning is very complicated; relying on three flat steels each reinforced with whalebone strips, which were added to the side seams of the garment. The closure on the busk is unusual as it features three retaining clasps to prevent it from opening.

Museum ref. B53

1903.

Kleinerts patent hook-on suspender attachment. The paired suspenders are made from 2.5cm plain elastic, the Fleurs-de-lys metal slides allowing them to be adjusted in length. The metal clip at the top hooked onto a busk stud at the centre front of the corset.

Museum ref. C25a

1903.

Short, high-waisted corset designed to fit low over the bust for eveningwear. In the first years of the new century evening gown necklines plunged lower and more revealing corsetry became necessary. The corset is supported by 36 whalebones and has a new, shorter busk.

Museum ref. C11

1903.

High waisted straight front corset in black sateen with distinctive white saddle stitching around each steel casing. There is curved hand flossing at the bottom of each steel. The corset is heavily boned with whalebone and flat steel.

Museum ref. C6

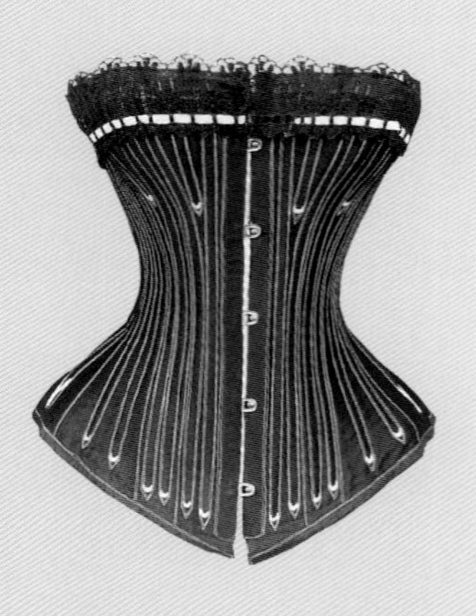

c1905.

Corset with a Y shaped busk which, in theory, left the lungs un-constricted whilst still supporting the bust. The principal of a divided busk at the top of the corset was first developed in the mid 1880s and was re-introduced in this garment which is made of pale green coutil and trimmed with blue corded satin and lace.

Museum ref. C22

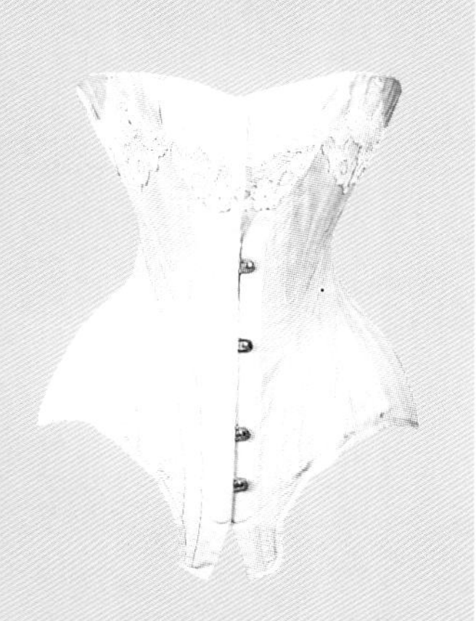

c1905.

Maternity and nursing corset. Back lacing and double side lacing with elastic sides for expansion during pregnancy. There is also an abdominal over-belt in elastic and cloth for support. Press-stud closing flaps allow the bust area to be opened for breast-feeding.

Museum ref. C27

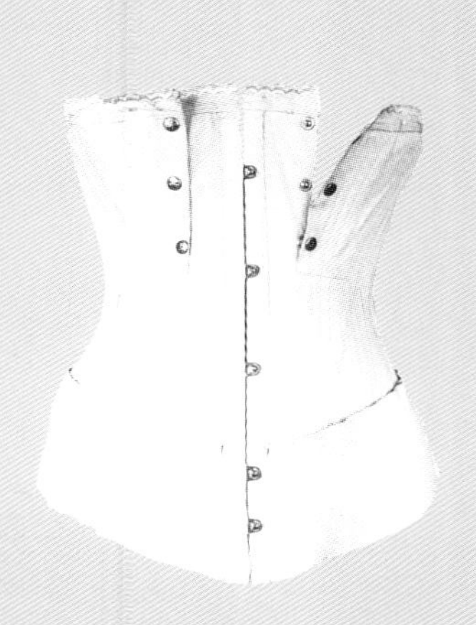

c1905.

Plunge front corset of black sateen, designed and made in France. The plunging front allowed some freedom for the bust but the heavily boned hips and waist pushed the body into the fashionable 'S' shape. The short, patent busk is lined with velvet to prevent rubbing.

Museum ref. C2

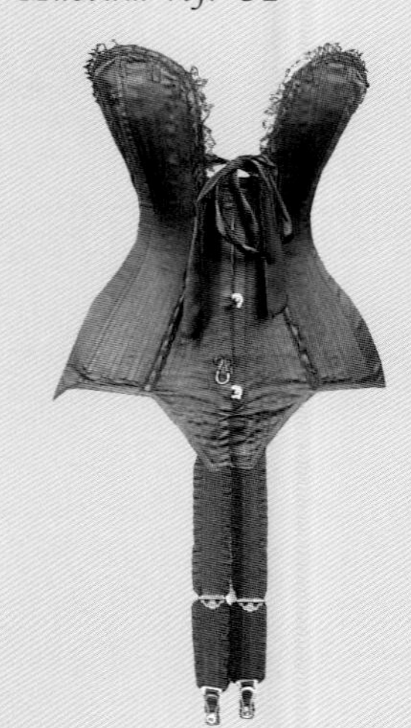

1908.

Straight front *'Health'* corset with a deep fitting under the bust and cut high over the hips.
The corset still fitted tightly at the waist and this style of garment was soon to be replaced by less restrictive, tubular garments.

Museum ref. C1

1908.

Printed Corset Box Top showing a straight front corset which gave the fashionable 'S' bend shape to a woman's body. The image gives a good insight into the combination of structured corsetry and softer underwear that was worn at the beginning of the twentieth century.
It is unlikely that the bust shape in this drawing could have been achieved without wearing a bust improver.

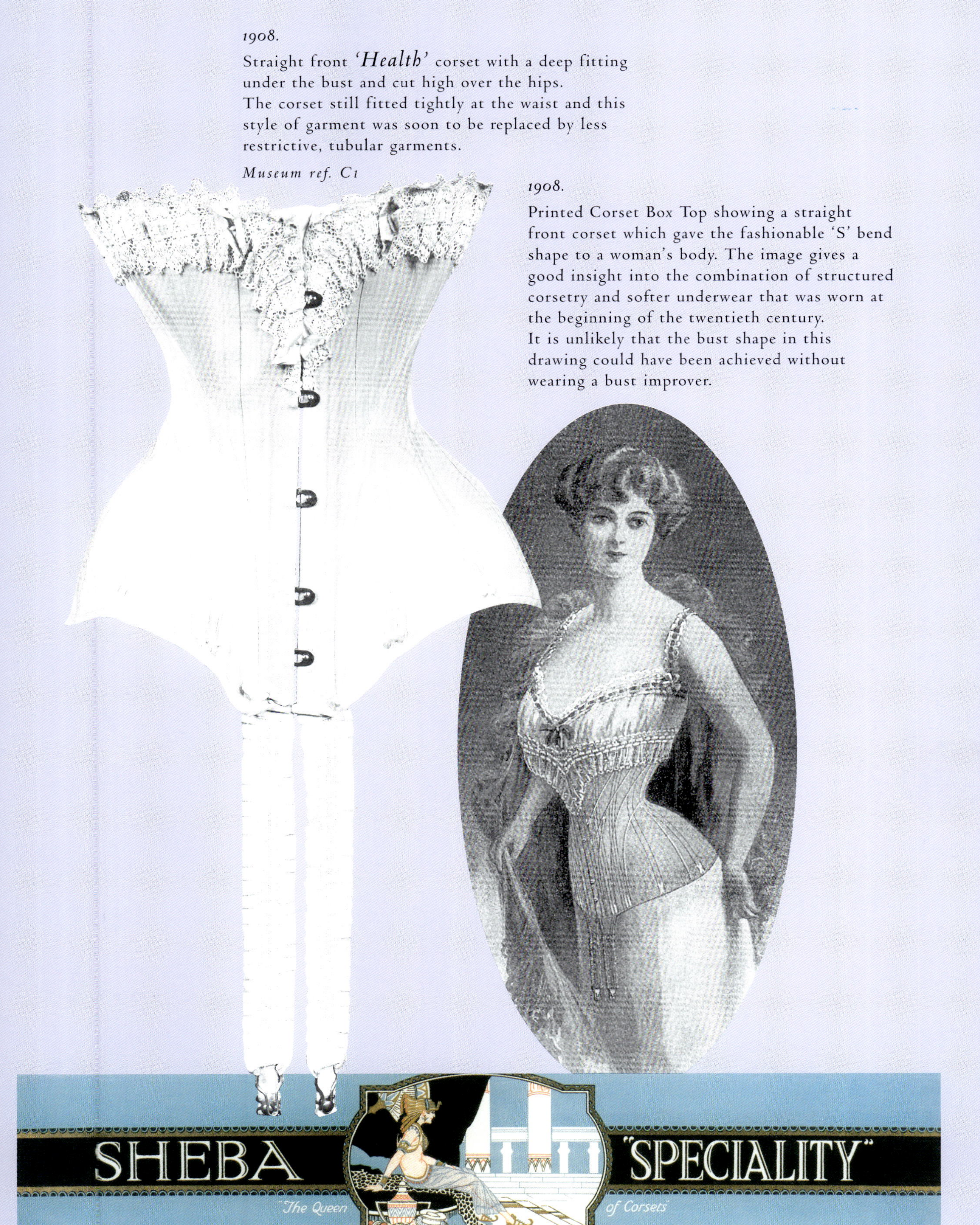

'Sheba' the Queen of corsets, a box top from around 1912, the design and colours show the influence of Paul Poiret's Orientalism.

1908.
'The Woven Waist' corset. The waist area is constructed with interwoven sections of superfine tape and woven cellular fabric across the hips. There are four attached elastic frilled suspenders.

Museum ref. C14

c1910.
'My Lady' corset made from dove-grey coutil. This straight front style features the new corset line giving a longer and more gentle curve at and below the waist. It has attached front and side suspenders and a new 'wedge' shaped busk fastening. The corset is supported with flat steel boning and stops below the hip. The top is decorated with a deep band of machine-made lace.

Museum ref. C5

c1910.
The forerunner of the suspender belt this hip corset has a press stud fastening at the front and lacing to adjust the fit at the back. There are four adjustable suspenders in frilled elastic at the centre front and sides. Even this lightweight garment is supported with twenty flat steels in double casings.

Museum ref. C69

c1910.
The *'Rational Corset Bodice'* is made from white cotton and is very lightly boned with removable steels, which allowed the corset to be laundered. It has button front fastening and laces down the back to allow for adjustment to the fit. This new lightweight corset was designed to give some degree of comfort and support and was marketed as being healthier than more constricting styles.

Museum ref. C4

COOK, SON & CO., LONDON.

"OKTIS" Shields.

When ordering your next parcel do not forget the "Oktis" with the Current Advertising Novelty. These are growing more and more into popular favour, the reason being that they undoubtedly perform what they claim, namely, double the life of a corset. Sold in two sizes.

No. 1. (Four Blades). No. 2. (Five Blades) or they may be had assorted.

Price 9/6 per dozen.

Less 1/- Coupon bonus which is to prevent price cutting

The *"Oktis"* corset shield, which had been advertised since 1897, here in an advert from 1912. The shield was supposed to lengthen the life of a corset by re-enforcing the boning at the front and side of the garment with a second layer of flat steels. These were stitched into the inside of the corset and give some indication of the wear that resulted from normal use. Even heavily boned corsets would suffer some 'fatigue', and the action of bending or stooping would, eventually break the bones of the garment.

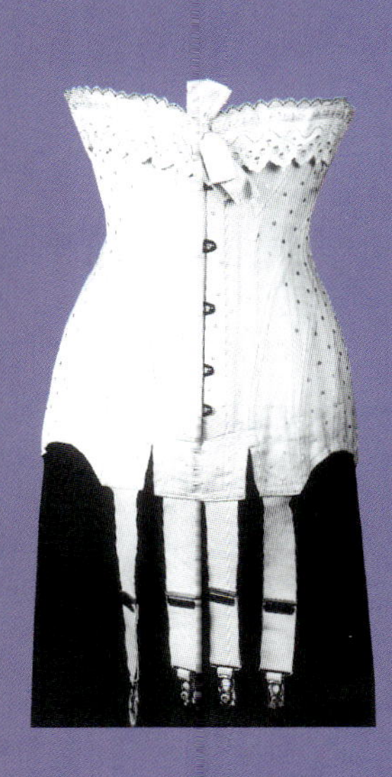

1911.
Straight front corset made in Belgium from white spotted cotton broche, trimmed with ribbon and Swiss embroidery. Although the corset is less restricting than previous styles it still uses a combination of whalebone and flat steel supports. The tapered busk is plush lined to prevent rubbing.
Museum ref. D41

1911.
French corset made from knitted tricot.
The stretching capacity of knitted fabric made garments like this a comfortable alternative to corsets that were made from woven fabric. Knitted tricot corsets were expensive and their price put them beyond the reach of most women. The laced back is selvedge-edged and has shaped panels to hold the ribbon-topped suspenders. The support for the garment comes from six sets of duplex steel boning.
Museum ref. D44

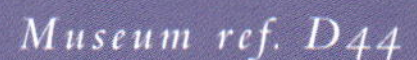

1914.
Ribbon corset with a low bust and lightweight skirt section. The bust section is constructed using lengths of broad brocade 'ribbon' or Barmen edging which allow for some freedom of movement and support. The boning is concentrated at the back and in the busk at the centre front.
Museum ref. D27

1912.
Catalogue illustration for the Jenyns' patent reducing and supporting corset.

The Jenyns' Patent Corset

THE MOST COMFORTABLE SUPPORTING AND REDUCING CORSET PROCURABLE.

AWARDED CERTIFICATE BY THE LONDON INSTITUTE OF . . . HYGIENE . . .

FOR HEALTH, FASHION AND HYGIENE . IT IS UNSURPASSED .

APPLIED IN ONE-HALF THE TIME AND WITH LESS LABOUR THAN ANY OTHER REDUCING CORSET

HIGHLY COMMENDED BY DOCTORS, NURSES, MATRONS, AND LEADERS OF FASHION IN THE . . LEADING COUNTRIES OF THE WORLD. . .

The Jenyns' Patent Corset Proprietary

321 George Street, Brisbane

1911.
Jenyns' corset designed in Australia and made under license by Symington. The corset has a distinctive back lacing belt section that was supposed to give 'increased ease in every position'. The Jenyns' lacing principle concentrated support along and across the lower back, while the front buckles allowed for the back control section to be pulled tighter adding extra support. Production of the Jenyns' style corset continued for many years and during World War One they were highly recommended for women engaged in war work whom, it was believed, required extra support for their backs.
Museum ref. D15

1913.
Catalogue illustration for *'La Contessa'* one of the very long corsets which gave the fashionable tubular silhouette of the period. Paul Poiret may have claimed that he had liberated women's waists from the shackles of a corset but his new column shaped woman wore a corset that constrained the hips and thighs making walking a difficult and often painful task.

Sporting Women

1890-1920

c1914.
The English sportswoman in some of her guises, from a Liberty Bodice show card.

c1900.

An avant-garde design for the sportswoman, this corset includes many features and adaptations to make it suitable for wearing for riding, cycling, tennis and golf. The corset is cut low under the bust to allow for full circular arm movement and high over the hip for riding side-saddle. The suspenders are attached and are very long. The boning is limited to the side seams, where it runs the full depth of the corset and the stomach panels where the boning is shorter and contained within the central section of the corset. The corset is very decorative and has a printed pattern of silver flowers on a black ground.

Museum ref. B33

c1900.

This corset is double laced down either side of a central metal busk. It also has lacing down the centre back.
The corset is heavily boned with 28 strips of whalebone but despite its restrictive construction was patented as having advantages for golfing and riding.

Museum ref. B37

c1905.

This riding corset is designed with the lower half of the back completely removed, allowing the rider to sit down with ease and comfort. The corset is heavily boned with a flared bust section narrowing to a tight waist. Riding habits were tailored and very tight fitting and a corset had to create a perfect figure that would be seen to advantage.

Museum ref. C84

1921.

Sports corselet made from white cotton batiste with a side hook and eye fastening and a short back lacing. The wide adjustable straps cross at the back and fasten to the front with rubber buttons. There are four attached suspenders.
Brief, lightweight garments such as these became popular in the 1920s when golf and tennis increased in popularity. The impact of sports corsetry on mainstream fashion can be seen in garments such as this, which set the style for later undergarments.

Museum ref. E15

The end of the nineteenth century saw dramatic and important changes in women's lives. 'The New Woman' emerged as a young, confident, educated, vital and pioneering spirit whose clothes reflected her new status and interests.

For decades sports such as riding, archery, croquet and even mountain climbing had been healthy pursuits for those women with money, leisure time and a spirit of adventure. As an increasing number of women took up sports such as golf, tennis and cycling specially designed clothes were produced to supply an eager market of sporting women.

One of the enduring images of the 'New Woman' of the 1890s was the cyclist whose image appears in advertising, cartoons, paintings, photographs and even popular songs of the day. Cycling became a craze and special clothes were designed for the comfort of the rider, these clothes included divided skirts and breeches, which caused a furore at the time.

Corsets were produced that were adapted for the fashionable sportswoman, many featured bust sections that were cut low under the arms, allowing the wearer full movement of her upper torso.
The skirts of the corset were cut high over the hips so that a woman could move her legs with relative freedom.

Sports corsets were some of the first to benefit from new fabric and fibre technology.
Although corsets with elastic had been shown at the Great Exhibition of 1851 they had never found a ready market until riding and other sports corsets featuring elastic panels were introduced in the 1890s.

Some elements of the design of those early sports corsets can be found in later fashionable foundation garments. The extra comfort and freedom of sports wear was popular with women who adopted some of its elements in their everyday dress. Some of the features that were incorporated into fashionable underwear include longer suspenders, elasticated panels at the diaphragm and shorter busks with simpler fastenings.

The success of the sports corset and its influence on fashionable foundation garments continued throughout the early part of the twentieth century. In 1912 the Liberty Bodice was produced in adult sizes; it proved popular with sportswomen and by 1915 was being specifically advertised as a sports garment.

The students of The Liverpool Physical Training College demonstrate the benefits of The Liberty Bodice for all manner of sporting activity. Shop show card from around 1914.

PLIO-TOP BUSK CORSET
SPIRAL STEELS

c1920.

Printed box top for *'The Royal Seal Sports Corset'* showing the classic women's sports of the age; tennis and golf.

c1905.

Advertising print showing a long fitting, straight-front corset with attached suspenders. The passion for exercise and sport amongst fashionable young women is clearly seen in this remarkable and, for its time, rather daring marketing image.

By the middle of the 1920s tennis and golf were accepted parts of many middle class women's lives and most would have owned a corset specially designed for the purpose.

A Revolution In Fashion 1915-1930

c1928.

Japanese inspired evening coat with deep fur collar and cuffs, showing the boy-slim silhouette and short length which were fashionable for the later years of the 1920s.

1917.

Austerity corset made in Germany during World War One. Acute shortages of materials across all the warring nations of Europe led to the development of new and unusual materials being used in corsetry. This corset is made from canvas-weave paper twine, which has been processed for rigidity and strength. What is also interesting is that a British company such as Symington managed to acquire an example of a German corset during the war.

Museum ref. D28

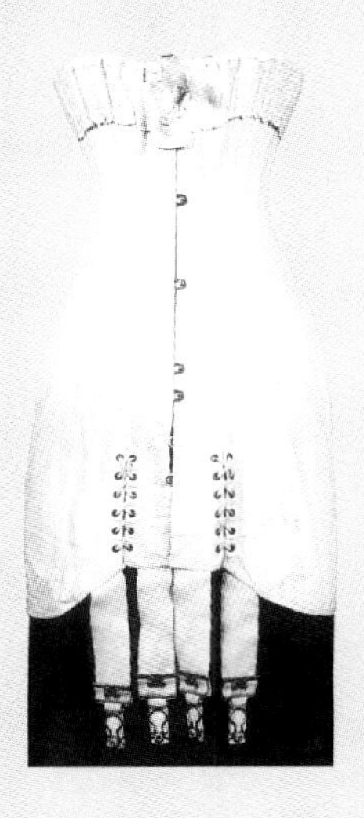

1918.

Deep busk front corset made in the U.S.A. The skirt of the corset is now at its lowest point in this model.
Steel boning runs down to below the hip giving control and support down the whole length of the upper body.
There are six sets of adjustable suspenders, the front four of which attach to an area which is adjusted by laces so that the extent of the wearer's stride could be controlled.

Museum ref. D39

c1920.

Early suspender belt in lined spotted shell pink broche.
The suspenders are a patent detachable style so that the belt could be washed without the metal and elastic parts.

Museum ref. D46

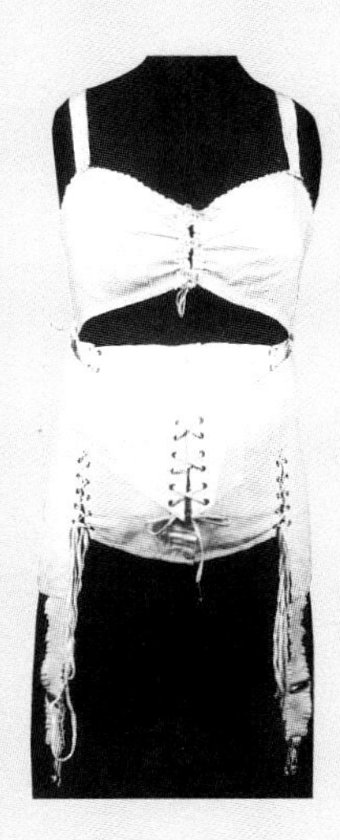

c1920.

Maternity corset made in Germany. This novel corset comprises a brassière and abdominal support section, which pre-dates the girdle.
The two sections join together with ties at the side seams of the waist. The brassière is adjustable at the centre front while the skirt section has three laced panels to allow for the development of the pregnancy. There is also extra support for the spine.

Museum ref. D23

c1920.

Young woman's suspender bodice made in Germany.
This lightweight garment is fully adjustable at the back, at the centre of the brassière section and at the shoulders, allowing for changes in the body shape, size and proportion during teenage development.
The buttons around the waist are for attaching to buttonhole drawers which were fashionable at the beginning of the 1920s.

Museum ref. D25

c1920.

Corselet bodice of pink fancy brocade trimmed with satin binding and machine lace.
This garment is designed and made for comfort and fashion, it has adjustable ribbon shoulder straps and a concealed front button fastening.
The style and comfort of the garment signals the movement towards more freedom-giving underwear.

Museum ref. D21

1921.

Maternity corset with elastic panels at the sides of the centre busk and lacing at the side seams. The elastic panels would have stretched with the developing pregnancy and lacing at the sides and back would have allowed for changes in the fit of the corset.
Despite this it would still have imposed a 'flat' tubular fashionable silhouette to a pregnant woman.

Museum ref. E17

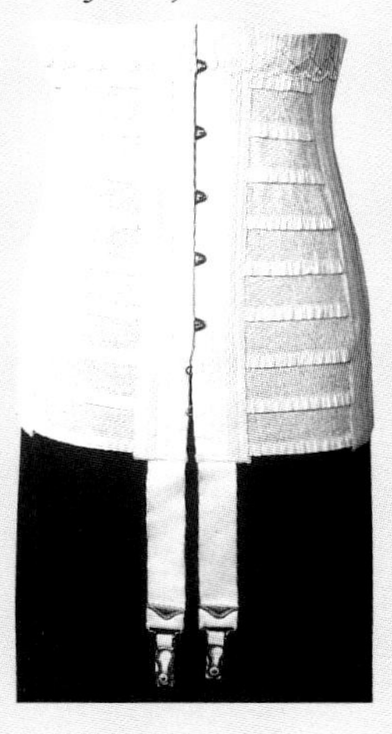

c1915.

An advert from a trade catalogue for the adult version of the Liberty Bodice, targeted at retailers who had contact with some of the many thousands of women involved in war work during World War One.

Museum ref. (D) Trade literature.

Any Ladies in your District Doing War Work?

If so, you have a good market for the

DEEP-FITTING Ladies'

Made in 5 sizes.	Prices.	Colors.
Small, Medium, Women's	3/11	Made in White and Natural.
Large, O.S.	4/6	

"Liberty Bodice" Factory, Market Harborough. (Wholesale only).

c1915.

From the same period, an advert for the Liberty Bodice this time targeted at the women themselves. In this case the marketing features all the benefits of the Liberty Bodice and clearly states that they come highly recommended by Doctors and Drill Instructors alike.

Museum ref. (D) Consumer literature.

Women who work

should not forego all support for their figures. The "Liberty Bodice" gives them entire freedom of movement with the right amount of support Carries all the weight of the underclothes and pull of suspenders from the shoulders. It also allows free expansion for breathing and promotes an easy grace. Flexible, porous and hygienic.

Highly recommended by Doctors and Physical Drill Instructors, for those interested in war-work, sport or gymnastics.

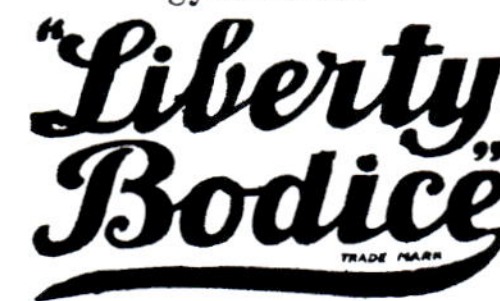

(KNITTED FABRIC)

Prices: Young Ladies', 2/11½ to 3/9; Women's (deep-fitting), 4/11½ to 5/9. Also in 13 sizes for Children: 1—3 years, 1/9½; 4—8 years, 2/3; 9—13 years, 2/6½.

Write for Free "Liberty Bodice" Book.

"LIBERTY BODICE" FACTORY, (Dept. 31a) Market Harborough.

The outbreak of war in 1914 was met with the usual waves of patriotic fervour in all the countries that were involved. It was however to be a war unlike any other, in which civilian populations were involved far more than ever before, where new technology was developed and harnessed and the world saw its first modern conflict. The social upheaval of the war and its aftermath brought changes to women's lives that would lead to the creation of the modern woman's wardrobe.

It is written in some fashion histories that during World War One women went out to work for the first time. In reality thousands of working class women had worked on the land, in industry and in service for centuries. What is true is that many thousands more, and for the first time large numbers of middle class women, went to work as part of the war effort. Women were called upon to work in factories, the transport industry, on the land and in other jobs that allowed men to go to the front. Those that weren't issued uniforms needed clothes that were practical, lightweight and easy to move in.

The demand for more practical clothing led to shorter skirts, which were fuller at the hem and allowed women to move with greater freedom. The waistline returned to its natural level and bodices, blouses and jackets were less restrictive especially at the shoulders, neck and across the bust and waist.

The corsetry industry went into full production making foundation garments that created a more natural figure but also gave support to the body, especially the back, during long hours of war work. Two garments produced by Symington stand out as being of particular importance during the period of the war.

In 1911 Symington began to produce the Jenyn's Patent Corset (see page 31) which featured a distinctive laced panel that supported the wearer's lower back. Although a pre-war development, the Jenyn's corset came into its own during the war as women engaged in war work were believed to be in need of extra support for their bodies.

Another pre-war invention that found favour with war workers was the Liberty Bodice of 1908 which was now made in adult sizes. It was warm, flexible and comfortable to wear, was relatively inexpensive and contained no metal parts, which were in short supply.

Drawings from 1920s show-cards, which would have been a feature of all large stores' corsetry departments and wall and window displays in smaller shops. The style of the drawings, which were thought to be preferable to photographs, reflected the design mood of the moment and featured a range of figure types and ages. The whole range for each season or year would feature in a large poster format. These store displays were incredibly important when different corsetry manufacturers were vying for the loyalty of the same customers.

Busk wraparounds from 1925.

Slipover bandeaux with elastic backs from 1922.

Diagonal front fastening brassière, 1923.

c1928.

'The invisible donor of outward and visible charm.' This marketing image for the Avro range makes the relationship between the foundation garment shown in the borders to the fashionable outer clothes presented in the middle of the picture.

The immediate post war period was a time of great success and expansion for R. & W.H. Symington. In 1922 the company opened a factory in Australia and production at home and abroad boomed. It was also a time of new challenges as traditional corset production began to decline and completely new styles of foundationwear had to be developed, manufactured, marketed and sold.

Women's outer fashion continued to develop along its freedom-giving lines. Clothes became simpler, lighter in weight, shorter and more fluid. Women were wearing clothes that weighed at least half as much as their pre-war counterparts. Chanel led the way in terms of design for those wealthy women who wanted fashion at its most modern.

New synthetic fabrics such as Rayon made clothes cheaper and easier to care for. This, coupled with simpler styles and improvements in the standard of manufacturing of mass-produced clothing, put fashion within reach of many more women. Paper patterns and simple styles led to a boom in home dress making and with a little flair a young woman could try to look like the models in the many women's magazines of the time.

Essentially the line of women's clothes was slim, flat and after 1925, short. New foundation garments created a tubular silhouette by flattening the bust and keeping the stomach, hips and bottom in line. The corsetry manufacturers began to use elastics, which had been significantly improved during the war, to create figure-controlling panels in the new, briefer corsets, wraparounds and corselets. Post war colours for foundation garments included 'butterfly blue', 'Persian mauve', 'shell pink' and 'wave green'. The corsets had to be very lightweight and sleek enough to fit underneath the flimsy outer garments without creating unsightly lumps and bumps. Traditional materials such as whalebone and cording were finally abandoned completely in favour of light-weight steels.

In 1923 R. & W.H. Symington introduced the 'Avro' range of foundation garments, their first, truly branded collection which included a full range of brassières, bandeaux, corsets (including sport and maternity corsets), corselets, wraparounds and health belts. Surprisingly the range was named after A.V. Roe a family friend who had been responsible for the development of Avro fighter planes which had achieved success in the wartime skies.

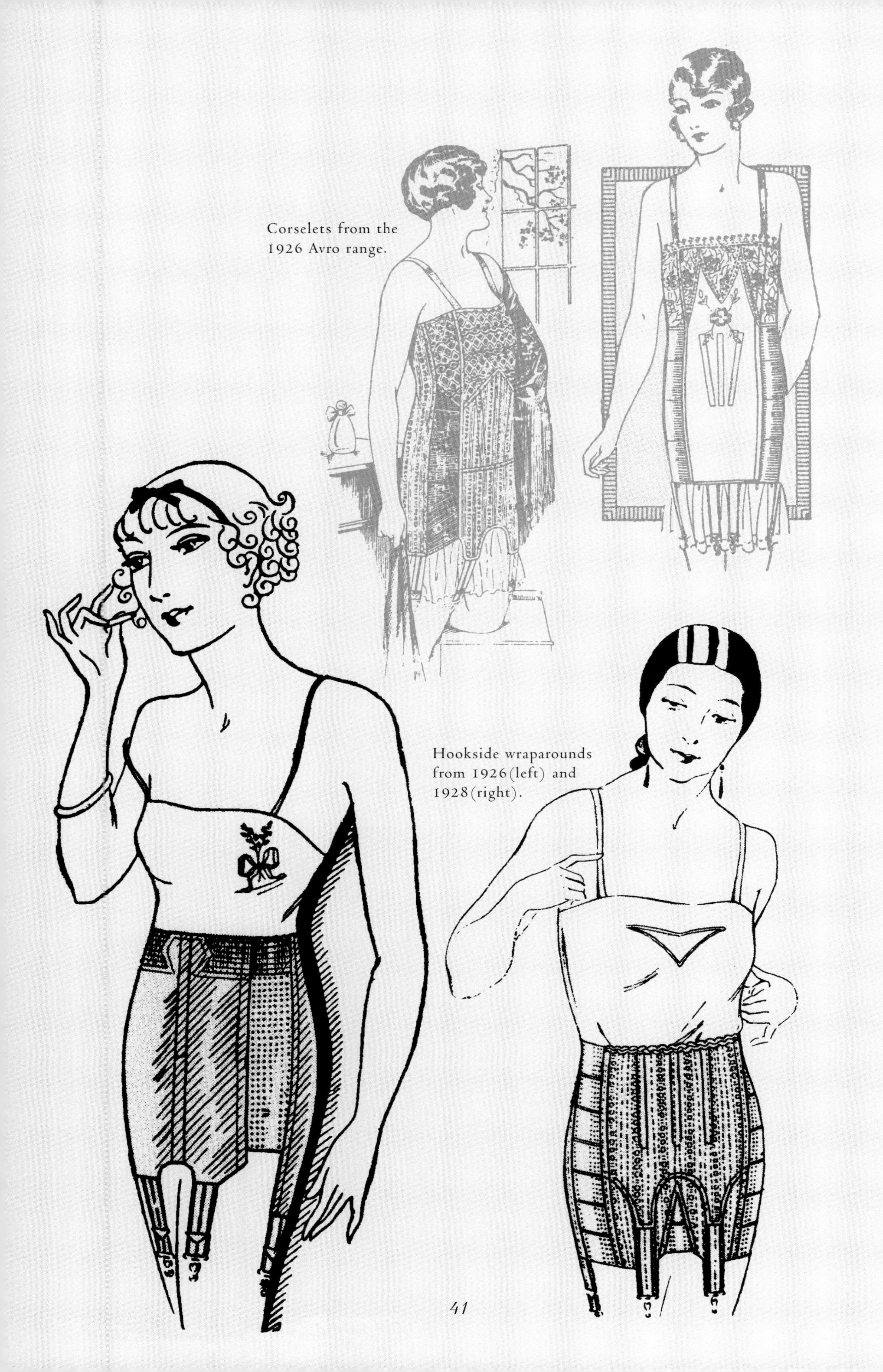

Corselets from the 1926 Avro range.

Hookside wraparounds from 1926 (left) and 1928 (right).

1928.
Marketing photograph for the Armmori Health Belt; a side closing girdle with stomach control panel and attached suspenders.

Museum ref. (E)
Trade literature

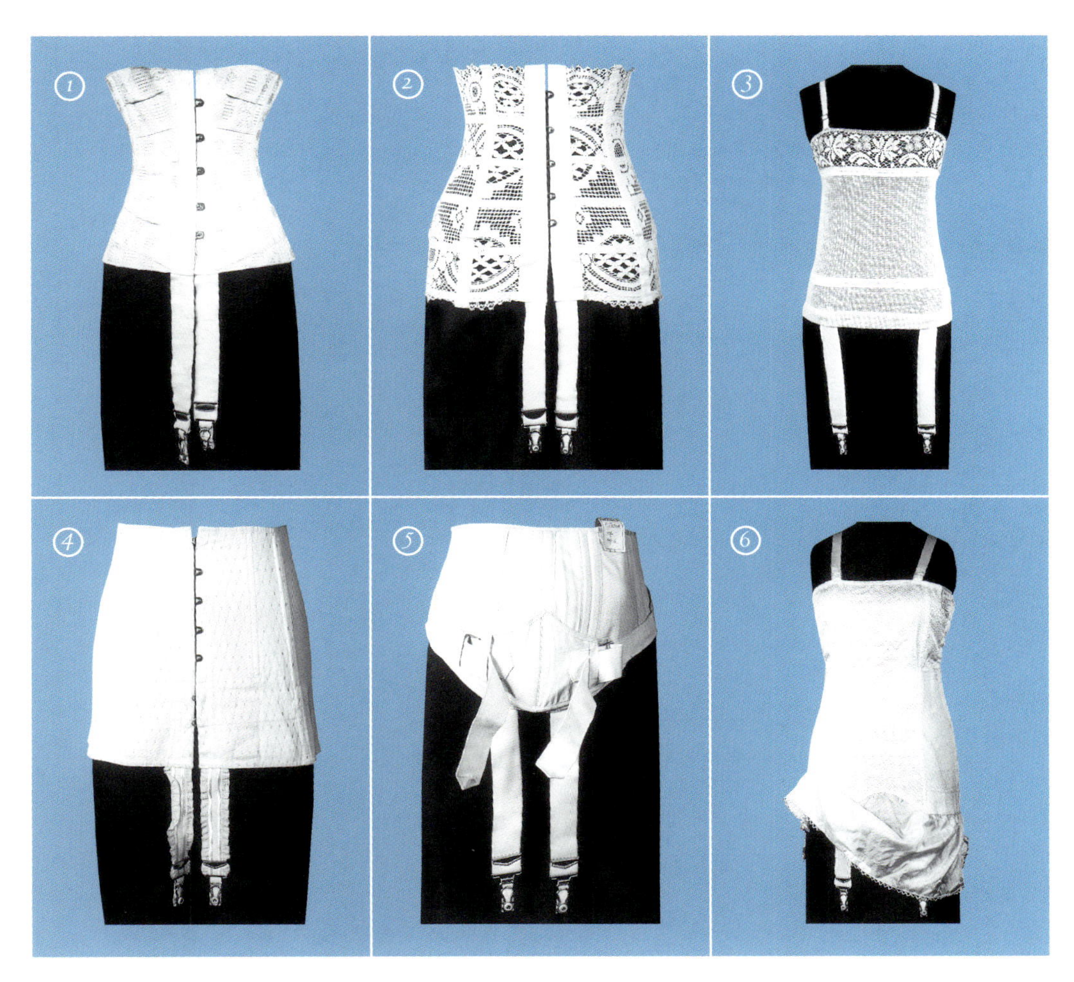

1. 1921.

Ribbon corset of blue and white 5cm Barmen edging. The ribbon strips allowed for much more movement especially at the top of the body. The shape is transitional between Poiret's long tubular silhouette and the boyish shape of the mid 1920s.

Museum ref. E7b

2. 1922.

Lightweight busk front corset made from panels of Cluny lace. The corset has small sections of boning in the side seams and the garment is supported with reinforced tapes running across the body to lightly control the figure.

Museum ref. E11

3. c1925.

All in one *'Sheathalo'* corset of knitted cotton tricot. The flat bust section is made from Cluny lace and there is no boning in the garment at all. Support and figure control came from the stretch properties of the knitted fabric.

Museum ref. E30

4. c1925.

Busk front wraparound. The advances in the development and production of elastic allowed deep, wide panels with powerful stretch and retention to be used in corsetry. This garment shows the transition from traditional busk-fronted corsets supported with boning to similar styles that make use of new textile technology.

Museum ref. E8

5. c1925.

Surgical support belt to provide abdominal support and figure control as well as acting as a suspender belt. The supporting webbing straps cross over at the back and return to the front where they are closed with buckles.

Museum ref. E41

6. 1928.

Corselet of white figured broche with crêpe de Chine skirt and detachable cami-knickers. This garment combines corset, knickers, slip and suspenders in one sleek piece of underclothing.

Museum ref. E37

Thirties Fashion

The return of feminine curves and a new longer length in this absinthe green coat by Chantal of Paris in 1933.

1934.
Avro Hookside wraparound in tea rose pink figured satin broche, with side panels of rayon elastic, lightly boned with flat steels. This model had one eye on value for money and retailed at the cheap price of 2s.11½d.

Museum ref. F12

1937.
An early colour photograph used to market the Avro range of foundation wear featuring the invisible studless fastener.
(See museum ref. F46 on p.48)

Avro
RECD.
Corsetry

GIRDLES

WRAPROUNDS

ACED FRONTS

CORSELETS

THE NEW INVISIBLE STUDLESS FASTENER

In 1929 the French fashion designer Jean Patou showed a collection in which he dramatically dropped the hems of the skirts to mid calf. The new longer length was met with widespread approval and both day and evening clothes became, and remained, long for much of the thirties.

At the same time Parisian designer Madeleine Vionnet was experimenting with creating clothes by cutting the fabric on the bias. Bias cutting means that clothes are cut using the cross grain of the fabric, they become more fluid and cling to the natural curves of the body. The look was particularly effective for eveningwear when satins and crêpes were cut into long, draped columns of fabric that clung to the breasts and hips and became fluid around the ankle.

Bias-cutting was revealing of the body, and worked to best advantage when falling over the body's natural curves. The slim, flat boyish shape of the mid 1920s gradually gave way to a fashion for a more curved, traditionally 'feminine' one. Bias cut fabrics reveal every lump and bump, not only of the wearer's body but also of whatever underwear they are wearing. For the foundation garment manufacturers this was important in two ways. First, women who had a less than perfect body required foundation garments that controlled their figures and presented a long, sleek, curved shape. This gave an opportunity to sell a variety of different types of foundation garments in a wide range of styles, to customers with an even wider range of figure types, ages and builds. Secondly, the manufacturers had to devise new ways of creating their foundation-wear so that it wasn't bulky, bumpy or heavy and did not show underneath the outer clothes.

By the early thirties the repertoire of R. & W.H. Symington encompassed hundreds of different sorts of garments. These ranged from traditional corset styles for older women with fuller figures to hookside and busk front wraparounds, corselets, medium, brief and deep brassières, roll on, zip and hook side girdles, suspender belts, sports-corsets, nursing and maternity corsets.

It was during this period that the brassière, or bra as it became known, came into its own. Bras of all types were introduced into the Symington ranges. They were of different styles and depths ranging from brief satin bras for younger women to wear with revealing evening dresses to fully boned bust bodices for women with larger busts. The adoption of the bra meant that full figure garments such as the corselet began to decline in popularity and briefer girdles and wraparounds increased as the garments of choice to be worn with a bra.

The garment types were available in a myriad of different styles, fabrics and in the three popular colours of the day, white, tea rose and pink. In 1938 there were more than fifty different types of brassière in the Avro range alone and the choice offered to the customer must have been mesmerising. The variations in design could be as slight as the depth of the strap that fastened a bra or the number of hooks on a corselet. Added to this the garments were available in a range of materials including cotton, rayon, silk, rubber and figured satins.

Elasticated fabrics developed very rapidly during the 1930s and their quality increased dramatically. In 1929 the Dunlop Rubber Co. introduced a new elastic yarn, evolved from latex, called Lastex. The development of Lastex meant that new elasticated fabrics could be made with a much finer texture and which benefited from two-way stretch. Lastex fabrics could be given the same surface treatments as other materials. Batiste, a strong elastic with a rich satin surface was particularly popular.

Rayon, which had been introduced by Courtaulds at the beginning of the century, reached the peak of its popularity during the inter-war years. It gave the visual effect of silk and was widely used for underwear especially in its knitted form 'Swami' for the cups of brassières.

The newly introduced elastic fabrics with their sleek and shiny finishes meant that smooth, slenderising underwear could be manufactured without resorting to rigid panels and heavy boning. The garments fitted so well that they hardly showed through the outer clothes. In 1937 Symington negotiated the exclusive rights to use E.W. Canham's patent slide-closing busk fastener which replaced the stud fastener and gave a smoother front to the corset.

c1935.
Suspender belt, first introduced in 1906, it proved unpopular and was withdrawn from the market. It was re-introduced in the late 1920s with enormous success, which peaked during the 1930s.
Museum ref. F17a

1934.
Hookside girdle featuring the NuBack panel which moved with the body when sitting or bending. Marketed as 'not riding up' the panel was cut quite low on the back, a feature which was appropriate for the low-backed style of gowns that were prevalent during the mid 1930s. The garment was moderately supported with flat and spiral steels and features the 'Concela' slides on its four suspenders.
Museum ref. F33

c1935.
Maternity hookside girdle in tea rose mercerised drill and plain cotton elastic. The whole front is elasticised and shaped to fit over the abdomen, there are three small bones, two at the base of the abdomen and one at the top. The girdle laces at one side and is lightly boned to support the back.
Museum ref. F44

1936.
Avro front lacing corset. This style was first introduced in America just before the First World War, but it was not until the mid 1930s that the style became popular and widely available in Britain. The corset was heavily boned with spiral steels making it suitable for women with a fuller figure.
Museum ref. F15

1937.
A wraparound featuring the new patent studless fastener designed to replace the conventional busk. E.W. Canham developed the slide closure and Symington negotiated its exclusive use on their garments on a royalty basis. It gave a more streamlined front to the corset and meant that dresses did not cling to the bumps of a traditional busk closure. Manufacturing was suspended during World War Two and resumed in 1949. By 1968 high production costs, and a change in underwear fashion stopped production altogether.
Museum ref. F46

1938.
'Slenderising' wraparound for the fuller figure in tea rose cotton-backed, perforated sheet rubber. After overcoming initial production problems, in which the seams gave way under tension, rubber foundation wear became popular in the late 1930s. Shortages of rubber suspended production during the war years and rubber corsetry never regained its popularity in the post-war period.
Museum ref. F18

1939.
Busk wraparound. Originally designed in the late 1920s, the busk wraparound became the natural successor to the heavier back lacing corset. The wraparound has a closed back and deep, elasticated side panels. This model features a short wedge-shaped busk, spiral steel boning and suspenders with the patent 'Concela' slides.
Museum ref. F2

1932.
Advertising drawing featuring the *'NuBack'* panel on a front fastening girdle. The picture shows the girdle being worn over a slip and with stockings.

Museum ref. (F) consumer literature

In 1932 the 'NuBack' panel was introduced under licence from the United States. This short panel, made with a semi-circular shaped hem, was fitted to the back of corsets and deep girdles. The elasticated sections prevented the corset from riding up in wear. It was applied to a large number of different corset styles and remained in production for over forty years

Two major innovations at the Symington Company were a new colour called tea rose and a completely new range of foundation wear called 'Liberty'.

Tea rose was introduced in 1932 and became immediately popular. It soon overtook the brighter pink of the 1920s in terms of sales and production.

The 'Liberty' range was a complete range of foundation garments that was produced alongside the Avro range. Liberty garments first appear around 1935 and production continued to increase steadily throughout the last years of the decade. Together with the 'Liberty Bodice' the Liberty range soon accounted for the bulk of Symington's production and the company had the word 'Libertyland' painted on the factory roof.

The Symington ranges went from strength to strength, comprehensiveness seemed to be the secret of their success, meeting the demands of all ages, figure types and budgets. Overseas production continued to grow. In 1934 a new factory in New Zealand joined the Australian branch opened in 1922 and in 1935 production began at Dundalk in Ireland.

It is fair to say that as the world moved towards war in 1939 R. & W.H. Symington could claim to make ready to wear foundation garments for almost every sort of woman whatever her age, size or income.

1. 1934.

Brief brassière with a new uplift design, made from two-way stretch Lastex net felled through with narrow fancy elastic. The straps are some of the first stretch models, in this case consisting of narrow eight-cord elastic. The bra fastens at the back with hooks and eyes.

Museum ref. F239

2. 1937.

Model suspender brassière in ecru needlerun lace lined with fine cotton net. Shaped at the front with darts and seaming, the bra finishes in deep points to which long narrow adjustable suspenders are attached. These brassières were first introduced in the early 1930s and were discontinued in 1939.

Museum ref. F320

3. c1935.

Deep brassière of tea rose pink brocade with wide central panel and high darted cups. The brassière closes at the side with six hook and eye fastenings and has ribbon straps, which could be adjusted by tying small knots in them. This is a transitional garment showing the movement from bandeau styles of the late 1920s and early 1930s and the cupped brassiere, which would remain popular for the next eighty years.

Museum ref. F249

4. c1937.

'Kestos' style bra from the Avro range in a double thickness of tea rose Celanese crêpe. The Kestos bra was very popular during the 1930s, being brief, light and comfortable. The simple cups were constructed with a single dart and the fit was adjusted across the back with crossover elastic straps that closed with buttons at the front. The top edge of the bra is overlocked with art silk thread.

Museum ref. F227

5. c1939.

Brief style brassière with multiple darted cups of tea rose 'Swami' the glossy knitted form of Rayon. The central panel is figured satin and the straps are made from 2cm ribbon. The bra closes at the back with a piece of elastic with hook and eye fastenings. 'Swami' was used extensively for bra cups as it was very soft and its glossy surface gave bras an air of luxury and exclusivity despite their very reasonable retail price of around 1 shilling.

Museum ref. F214

6. c1939.

This deep, button through brassière with its built up shoulders, elastic straps and diaphragm panel was marketed to women with a fuller figure. The garment is made from cotton with plastic buttons and 5cm elastic straps that attach at the centre back. The elastic tab, with its metal loop was designed to fix the bra to the busk fastening of a corset or girdle to prevent the brassière from riding up.

Museum ref. F284

Fashion On The Ration

1940-1947

1940.
Hookside corselet with a deep under-belt in tea rose pink figured batiste.
The bra section has deep uplift cups with ribbon shoulder straps attached to elastic. The hookside corselet was to become the 'all-in-one', and would retain its popularity throughout the next twenty years.
Museum ref. F52

"Make do and Mend" was the ethos of fashion during World War Two.
Stitchcraft Magazine, December 1941.

One of the competition... but this advert for Berlei corsets from 1941-42 shows two of the pressures that women on the Home Front felt; comfort and proper support during the long hours of war-work and keeping the morale of the nation's men high by presenting a fashionable and attractive figure.

The outbreak of World War Two in September 1939 was to have a dramatic effect on all aspects of life in Britain. Being an island that had, before the war become dependent on imported goods from all over the world the country found itself suddenly isolated from its international suppliers. Blockaded from the outside world, Britain was only able to import vital supplies in heavily defended ocean convoys that were constantly under attack. All goods were in short supply, but luxury goods were almost impossible to get hold of. For most people the war years were exhausting and putting food on the table and clothes on their backs was a constant struggle.

The fashion and beauty industry was an important part of the war effort. Some high fashion collections were created for export in exchange for much needed foreign currency. It was also believed that the country needed to keep its morale high and women's fashion, and their appearance in general, was thought to play an important part in this. The nation still needed to be clothed and new styles were designed that used less fabric, which was in short supply, and took less time to make, so saving valuable factory production time.

Despite, and sometimes because of, the shortages there were definite new styles of dressing for women. Skirts became shorter and narrower, with false pleats and pockets. There was little applied decoration but colourful printed dress fabrics were popular. Shoulders were padded and slightly square, jackets were narrow and short. A few women wore trousers, partly from practicality but also because stockings were in very short supply. Underwear such as French-knickers, slips and underskirts were sometimes made from parachute material.

Millions of women helped with the war effort, working in factories, on the land, in hospitals and in the armed forces. Called up to the war effort and working long hours in their homes, women were told that they needed strong foundation garments to support their bodies especially their backs.

Life at R. & W.H. Symington was also affected. During the war 156 people from the company joined the forces; six of them never returned. Some of the factory itself was given over to war production including the sewing of shirts, shorts, sand-fly and mosquito nets for the desert and jungle campaigns. Much of the factory was involved in the making of parachutes, over a million in all, using 25,000,000 yards of silk and 65,000,000 yards of cord.

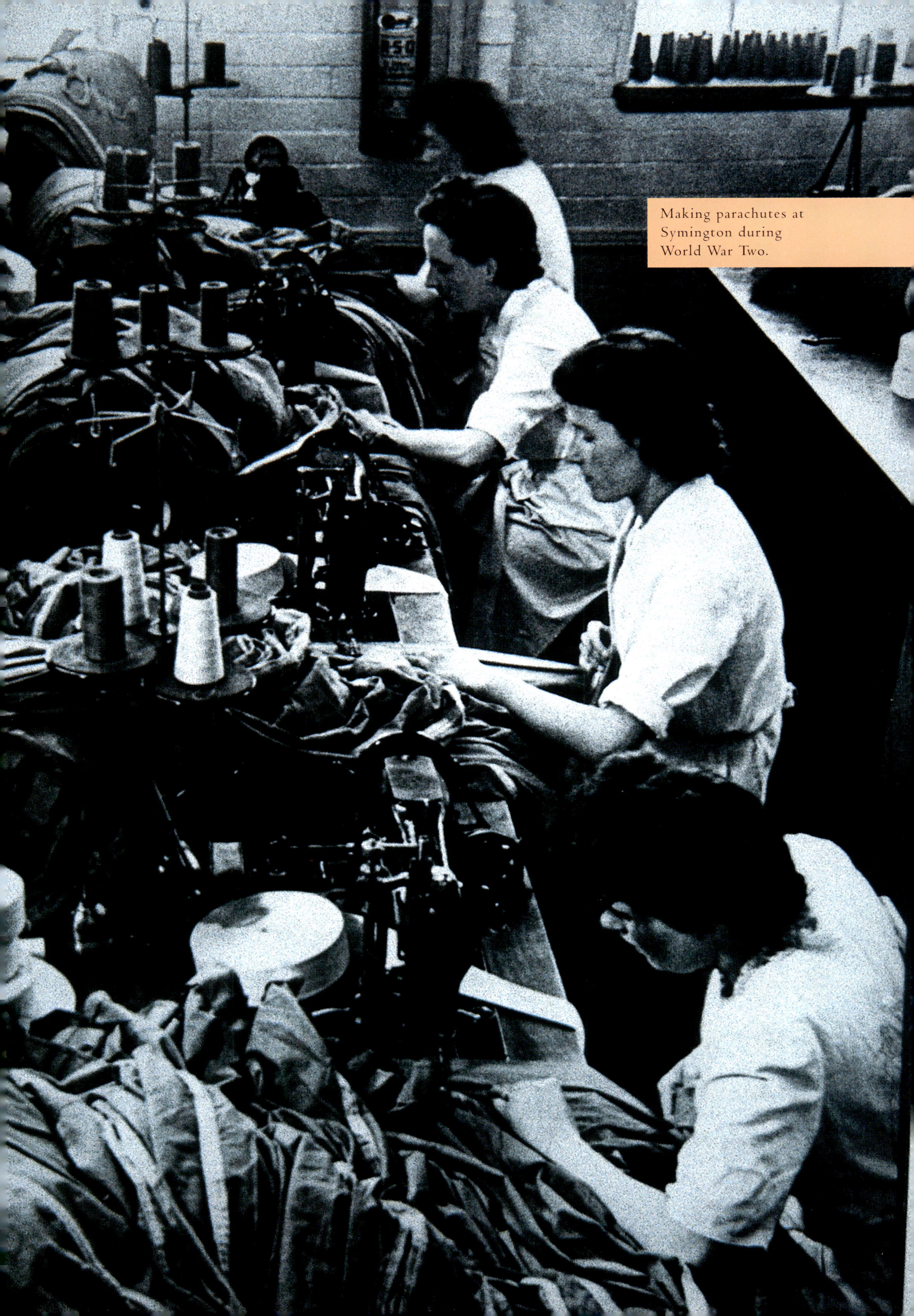

Making parachutes at Symington during World War Two.

1. 1941.

Avro busk wraparound in tea rose broche with rayon elastic panels across the top at the front and bottom at the back. This model was first introduced in 1932 and was modified for production under the Utility regulations.

Museum ref. G20

2. 1941.

Maternity girdle in tea rose pink cotton drill with a shaped elastic panel at the front. There is a hook and eye fastening at each side with lace adjustment to allow for the development of the pregnancy. Introduced during the war years this model remained in production until 1968.

Museum ref. G3

3. 1941-1942.

This busk front, laced back corset has a deep under-belt which also has a busk front closure making it highly constricting. Ideal for the fuller figure it contained spiral and flat steel boning and broad panels of elastic.

Museum ref. G16

4. 1943.

Hookside corselet in cotton collar cloth with cotton poplin uplift bust sections. This model features a hookside, lightly boned under-belt.

Museum ref. G17

5. 1943.

Hookside girdle in tea rose pink broche with rayon elastic panels and insets. Designed for the slimmer figure this model featured control which was created with elastic only. Later cotton-backed versions included flat and spiral steel supports for larger women.

Museum ref. G2

6. 1943.

Avro front lacing corset in tea rose pink strong collar cloth with elastic insets. It was heavily boned with a combination of flat and spiral steels. Government restrictions also permitted this model to be made in broche.

Museum ref. G8

Government Board of Trade directives outlining the regulations for the production of clothing and corsetry during the Second World War. All fashion companies had to comply with the Board of Trade regulations which were constantly being revised and re-issued. To the right is the card which Symington produced to celebrate the end of the war in 1945.

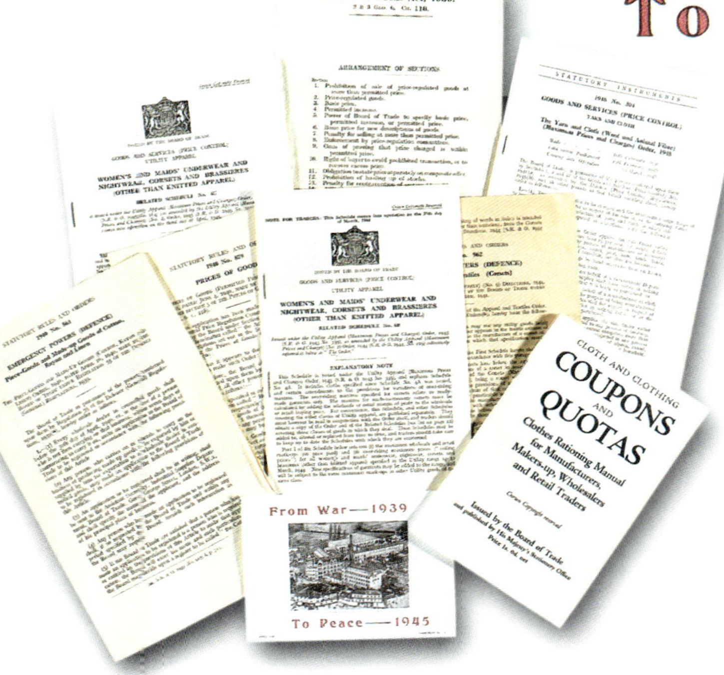

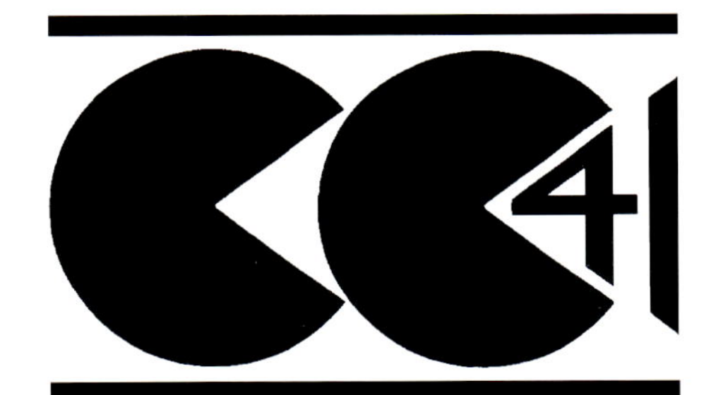

The Utility symbol, introduced by The Board of Trade in 1941, which had to be marked on all garments and packaging that were manufactured under Utility regulations.

From June 1941 clothing was strictly rationed, each adult was issued with 66 clothing coupons a year. Each garment had a standard coupon value that had to be handed over at the time of purchase. Rationing was supposed to ensure a fair distribution of scarce clothing supplies but for most people brand new clothes were a rare luxury. Traditional skills of sewing, knitting and dressmaking came into their own as housewives all over the country were exhorted to 'make do and mend' repairing old clothes and making new ones from whatever could be found.

In 1941 the Board of Trade introduced the Utility scheme which prescribed the amount of material, type of decoration and length of time in manufacturing that every different type of garment could have. The regulations extended to the manufacture of corsetry and also limited the type of fabric that a particular corset style might be made from. Garments produced under the scheme all bore its distinctive mark.

Silver grey shantung dupion silk suit by Dorville, Spring 1953.

In February 1947 Christian Dior launched his first fashion collection in Paris. Called 'The Corolle Line', and dubbed the 'New Look' by American Vogue's Carmel Snow, Dior's vision of a post-war woman was an elegant, corseted figure with gently sloping shoulders, a small waist, padded hips and a skirt falling to just above the ankle.

Compared to the shorter, more economical designs of the war years the 'New Look' was dramatically different. Most of the world was still reeling from the effects of the war, there was rationing in Britain, food shortages in France and millions of displaced people all over Europe. Women who had grown used to being at work and earning their own salaries found themselves 'encouraged' to return to the home as men came back from the war to search for employment. Against this background the Edwardian styles from which Dior drew his influences seemed strangely at odds with life in 1947. The 'New Look' was attacked from all sides; by politicians who doubted its economic sense at a time of critical shortages, by women who thought that it was retrograde and impractical and by others who thought that the long skirts denied women's sensuality by hiding their legs.

And yet, despite it all there was something in the glamour and romanticism of the 'New Look' that captured thousands of women's imaginations and they did everything that they could to get it. At 40,000 French francs for a dress there was only a handful of women in the world who could afford a real Dior. The war time ethos of 'make do and mend' was still strong; women took panels of fabric and added them to existing skirts to make them longer; two dresses were combined into one to make a fuller skirt. Many sets of blackout curtains, discarded after the war, were transformed into 'New Look' suits and coats.

The 'New Look' silhouette could only be achieved by using a foundation garment that created a small waist, emphasised the hips and produced a high, rounded bust. Dior created his own corset in silk with ruffles at the bust and horsehair frills at the hips. The silhouette was an elegant hourglass and, with minor changes, was to persist throughout the 1950s A tightly fitted bodice or suit jacket, a small waist, a definite exaggeration of the hips and a long skirt that was either very full or pencil slim was to be the fashionable ideal for nearly a decade. Evening dresses were either romantic, with bell-shaped skirts or dramatically sensual, tight fitting columns.

While minor changes in the hem lengths of Paris fashion made the front pages of daily newspapers they didn't affect the overall figure shape of 1950s women.

For R. & W.H. Symington the 'New Look' silhouette was an important development. It meant that there was a huge market for new foundation garments that used some elements of 1890s corset design but that were made in the modern fabrics of the post war technology boom. Nylon was extensively used in many of the garments not only in flat and figured fabrics but also in lace, net and stretch fabrics. The new nylon fabrics were strong, fine in texture and responded well to washing and wear. In 1955 polyester was introduced under the brand name Terylene and was used for rich jacquards and satins.

In 1952 the Utility scheme was finally abandoned and full production of completely new garments, particularly in the 'Liberty' range, began. Women had a huge amount of choice and they were encouraged to buy new foundation garments in a series of widely publicised fitting weeks throughout the mid 1950s.

By the middle of the decade it was obvious that there was a growing market of young people who had begun to dress, socialise and behave in a different way to their parents' generation. No longer children, teenagers were demonstrating that they had new interests and lifestyles and that they had spending power. New outer clothes, heavily influenced by American youth culture and Hollywood teen movies, meant that young women wanted new underwear. Symington began to produce attractive matching sets of bras and suspender belts in pretty colours that were daintily decorated. The 'Avro Petites' range was introduced in 1958 with a clever advertising campaign that treated its customers, who would have previously been thought of as children, like adults. The range was an instant success with the new generation of young, fashionable women.

By now most women found the bra and girdle the most important foundation garments and they were produced in a wide variety of styles, fabrics and colours (including black). In 1956 cup sizes were introduced for bras, although there was no standardisation between manufacturers, and the new measurement, 'hip spring', became an important feature of design and fitting. Hip spring was the difference between the waist and hip measurements; a woman with a 26" waist and 38" hips had a hip spring of 12".

1952.

The Très Secrète inflatable bra, introduced into Britain from the United States by La Resista Corset Co and made under licence by Symington. The marketing of the très secrète was a collaboration between Symington and Supportu Supplewear a wholesale distribution company based in Wigston, Leicestershire.

Originally marketed as a fashion brand, when the ideal woman had the figure of Jayne Mansfield or Marilyn Monroe, the très secrète later found most of its market in women who had undergone mastectomy.

Museum ref. H250

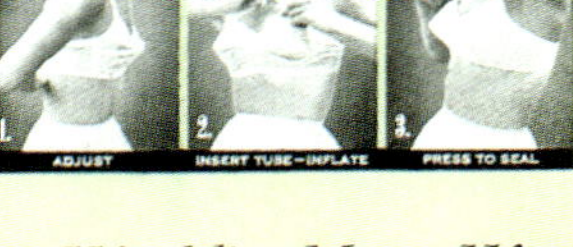

Price 2 guineas
A & B cup fittings.
White. Sizes 32, 34, 36.

It's the World's Most Wanted Bra!

So very comfortable

By giving you the right support a Liberty foundation helps you to sit and stand with a straight back. In this way it rids you of those little aches and pains caused by slumping when you are tired. Whether you choose a Liberty Lace-up, or a cleverly boned step-in, see just how very comfortable they can be.

For a smooth figure line

Whether you have a short, tall, or full figure, there's a Liberty to give you the control you need to wear the slim-fitting clothes you love. For the dress that needs a smooth unbroken line from the bosom to the thigh, there are sleek, slenderising Liberty corselets. For the dress that calls for a well-controlled waist and midriff, there are high-waisted step-ins. Look too for the garments with the exclusive NUBACK and NUEASE Panels. They're blissfully comfortable and specially designed for the fuller figure.

Moving freely

One of the features that has made Liberty so famous is NUBACK (see p. 17). This ingenious free moving panel prevents any irritating riding-up no matter how active your life may be.

Keeping trim

Even if you're slim and perfectly proportioned you still need a foundation for the support it gives to the muscles (especially the stomach muscles) will help to keep your figure trim. In any case, an uncontrolled figure can never look really elegant and with any fashion you must have a smooth outline, well-controlled hips and a flat tummy. You'll find that a Liberty will give your figure a lovelier line by controlling correctly and without discomfort.

1954.

Symington appeals to two areas of its market in this catalogue spread from the mid 1950s. The smart older woman who sought to retain her fashionable figure with some element of comfort and the younger woman who wanted freedom of movement coupled with a seductively slim silhouette.

Trade and consumer literature from the Liberty range, which accounted for most of Symington's production during the 1950s. The design and marketing departments were at their most prolific and sophisticated during the 1950s, producing glamorous and well conceived literature, advertisements and television commercials.

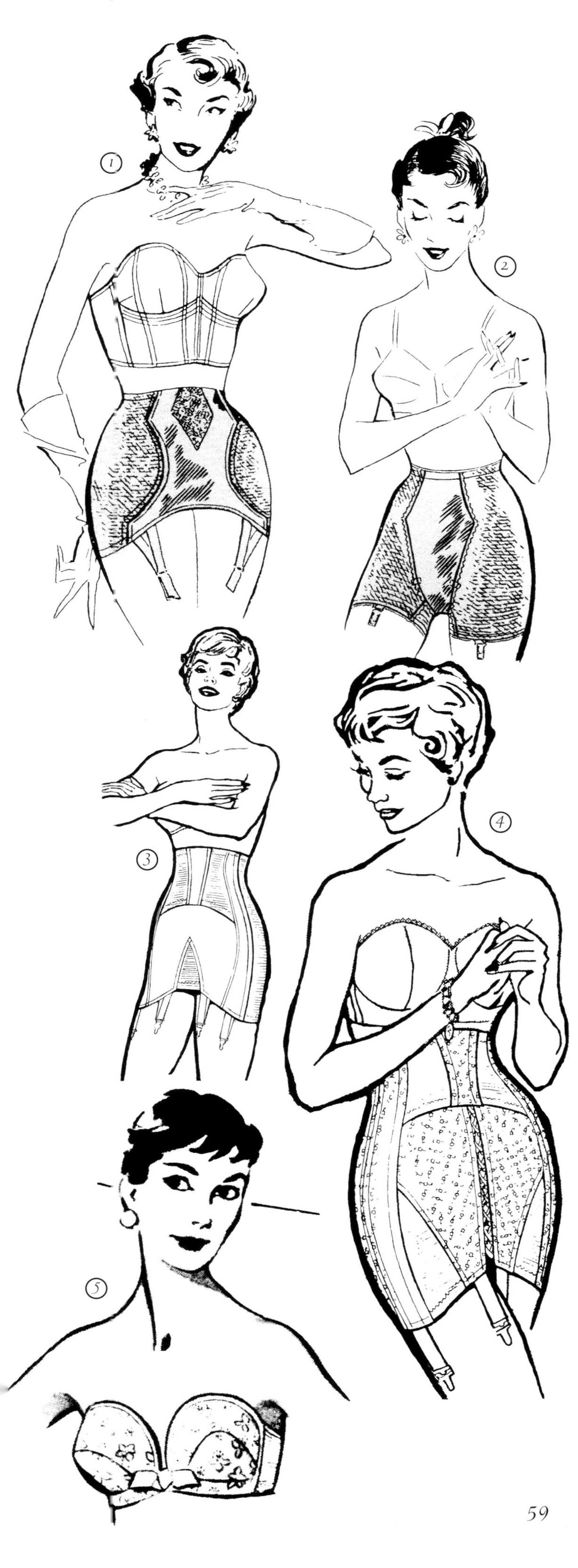

1. 1952.

A freedom giving pull-on girdle designed in white cotton, rubber, nylon and elastic net with a deep cut-away front in cotton lined satin and lace. This style of pull-on garment became very popular in the post-war period when women's fashion, and especially 'occasion' clothing, demanded a very exaggerated curved figure.

Museum ref. H5

2. 1952.

An early 1950s Liberty pantie girdle in white nylon, elastic net and satin Lastex. It has a deep elastic waistband stitched inside and there is a detachable rayon gusset lining.

Museum ref. H6

3. 1954.

Liberty *'NuBack / NuEase'* hookside girdle, one of Symington's most successful products of the period. This lightweight but hardwearing garment was advertised on television, in the press and in women's magazines. It features the NuBack panel, which was first introduced in the 1930s. The NuEase panel in the front of the garment moved downwards as the wearer stooped forward so that the steels did not poke into the diaphragm.

Museum ref. H10

4. 1954.

Liberty high waisted corset in tea rose pink two tone figured batiste. The front lacing corset became available in a much lighter form. This high waisted style had several new features including elastic panels and side hook and eye fastening.

Museum ref. H42

5. c1955.

Brief strapless bra in a wired plunge design. The cups are formed from a figured Terylene polyester with satin covering for the wiring. The back fastens with a four way adjustable eyelet system on an elastic strap. The deep plunge, coupled with the strapless design gave this model little success as it slid down the bust giving no support.

Museum ref. H200

6. 1957.

Brief underwired bra in white nylon lace and marquisette. This fashion bra features the new Velcro fastening at the back.

Museum ref. H242

1958-1960.

The Liberty *'Topliner'* high waisted step-in girdle with side zip fastener and matching bra. This marketing photograph is interesting in that the underwear has been painted onto the photograph to give a more 'perfect' image of the range.

Museum ref. H78

1959.

This high waisted semi step-in has a central zip fastening and is made from Bri-nylon and elastic net. Its central panel is of nylon voile with lilac embroidery. The matching bra has removable straps and retailed at 23s.6d.

Museum ref. (H)
Consumer literature

The Liberty range accounted for most of Symington's production during the 1950s. The design and marketing departments were at their most prolific and sophisticated during the 1950s, producing glamorous advertisements such as this one from 1953.

There was a great emphasis on the bust in fashion design throughout the 1950s. Dresses, jackets and sweaters were designed to be close fitting and showed the breasts to full advantage. Hollywood stars such as Marilyn Monroe, Jane Russell and Jayne Mansfield became the pin-ups of the decade and their figures became the ideals of the day.

Spiral or circle-stitched bras gave a prominent shape to the bust, wiring and boning lifted the breasts and pointed them outwards and some women padded their bras with tissues to give a more ample affect. 'Falsies', small pads that were fitted into the bra cups, sold in their thousands and bust shape became an obsession for some women. In 1952 the 'Très Secrète' inflatable bra was introduced into Britain.

The 'Très Secrète' was designed by La Resista Corset Co. of Bridgeport in the United States. Symington agreed to manufacture the bra under licence with Supportu Supplewear Co. of Wigston acting as sole distributor. The bra was of conventional design but had pocket linings in each cup. Small plastic pads were inserted into the pockets and these were inflated by blowing through a small straw when the bra was put on. When the cups had been inflated to the correct size, the straw was removed, and the valve sealed by pinching it together between the thumb and forefinger.

Many women bought the 'Très Secrète' simply to improve the shape or increase the size of their bust. For others it was important as a post-operative bra after breast surgery.

In 1957 Symington won the licence to produce ready to wear foundation garments for Christian Dior. The range was designed in outline in Paris but much of the work was done in Symington's own design rooms incorporating the key elements of Dior's designs. There were certain 'signature' elements in the range, which was available in black, and white with sugar pink trimming. Each garment had a lattice of velvet ribbon running down the centre front panel and some had elastic panels woven with Christian Dior's initials. Bras that were boned were lined with velvet to prevent rubbing and all of the range featured the recently introduced velcro fastening. The range was very exclusive, selling in stores such as Harrods and Selfridges in London. The collection was launched at the Savoy hotel, London in September 1957 and Dior himself was meant to attend. Unfortunately Dior was ill and died within a month.

The range was successful but difficult and expensive to produce. It had a limited market and the volume of stocks and the supply of materials from France became problematic. In 1959 production was transferred to Alcock and Priestly Ltd. a subsidiary company of R. & W.H. Symington.

The end of the 1950s brought the end of the Dior collections at Symington. It had been a decade dominated by the elegant, suave, ultra-feminine figure that Dior had created in 1947. Symington had harnessed new technology and new marketing techniques to produce and sell some of its most effective foundation garments, but it was to find the next decade to be one of new challenges and dramatic changes.

1959.

Christian Dior corselet in jacquard elastic net and nylon. The lattice bands of pale pink velvet over a panel of white nylon lace were the signature of Dior foundation wear. The Dior underwear range was targeted at an elite market, which was reflected in the cost of the garments - this corselet sold for £7.19s.6d.

Museum ref. H54

Sixties & Seventies

'Dandy' a red and white candy stripe wool trouser suit designed by Anthony Charles at Koupy 1967.

Reproduced by kind permission of the Woolmark.

1961.

Suspender belt and matching bra in white nylon and pink rosebud-flocked voile from the Avro Petites range. Matching sets were a particularly successful part of the teenage ranges produced by Symington in the late fifties and early sixties. The advent of tights and trousers made the suspender belt a redundant piece of clothing as far as the majority of young women were concerned.

Museum ref. J58a and J201

The 1960s and 1970s were a time of huge changes in the world of fashion design, the social and economic life of women and in R. & W.H. Symington as an organisation.

The growth of the youth market, which had begun to develop in the middle of the 1950s, gathered momentum in the next decade. By 1965, teenagers and young adults were a powerful force in the fashion and leisure industries. Young women in particular had spending power and more freedom to choose how to use it. Fashion designers such as Mary Quant and Courrèges created clothes that focused on a new, younger woman. The fashion fabrics of the day were new, robust synthetics and bonded jerseys that stood away from the body when cut in flat, geometric planes. Styles were short and for the first time Paris Couture showed skirts above the knee. New forces drove fashion; the aristocratic restraint and elegance of the 1950s gave way to a vital, energetic 'youth-quake'. There were new stars to admire; The Beatles led the world of popular music, models such as Twiggy and Jean Shrimpton influenced the way that women wanted to look. Vidal Sassoon revolutionised everybody's idea of a haircut and Carnaby Street became a mecca for the young and fashionable.

As far as fashion was concerned the major influences were those designers who created collections for the youth market and the styles that they set impacted on the foundation wear industry. The mini skirt, the defining piece of clothing of the sixties, brought an enormous change to women's underwear. Stockings, which under a mini skirt revealed bare thighs, became impractical and the invention of tights meant that the suspender belt, a staple for the Symington Company for over thirty years, fell out of fashion almost over night. Suspenders were eventually removed from almost all but the most traditional of Symington's ranges.

Perhaps the other most startling change to fashion was the steadily increasing acceptability of trousers for women. The trouser had the same impact on foundation garments as tights had on the suspender. For many years, girdles and corselets had been skirted. These styles would not fit underneath trousers and the pantie-girdle and pantie-corselet became immediately popular.

The pantie-girdle controlled the hips and stomach and fitted between the legs with a gusset. All-in-one garments that controlled and reduced the figure could give a slimmer silhouette at a time when the unusually thin model Twiggy was the ideal of the day. Many women dieted to achieve the skinny look of the moment but for many more, controlling fashionable foundation garments were a means of creating a slimmer figure.

Early in the 1960s Du Pont introduced Spandex, which it had developed in 1959. Spandex (later known as Elastane) could be made into a power-net with multi-stretch and tremendous recovery. Under the trade name Lycra, the new fibre became an integral part of the new foundation garments that were being produced. Other new fabrics quickly followed, including soft stretch tricots, which could be printed and matched to other garments to create co-ordinating sets of underwear. New printing technologies created fashionable psychedelic patterns and underwear entered a new age of colour and surface decoration.

Popular since the 1930s, the bra had become the fundamental foundation garment that most women wore, so much so that it became a symbol of oppression for the developing women's liberation movement of the late 1960s and early 1970s. Bra design and manufacture became increasingly sophisticated and ranges of different styles were created. New technology meant that bra cups, which had previously been made up from several small and complicated pattern pieces, could now be moulded and lined in a process called 'pre-forming'.

In 1967, after over one hundred years of family control the company was taken over by the textile giant Courtaulds and a new era began at the factory.

From the late 1960s and throughout the 1970s Symington produced garments for the major retailers of the day including 'St Michael' for Marks and Spencer, Dorothy Perkins and 'Keynote' the brand name for Littlewoods. The Mothercare store group was supplied with maternity and nursing underwear, particularly bras, and also with swimwear and nightdresses. The making of garment ranges under other companies' brands continued on alongside Symington's own brands, Liberty, Eros and Peter Pan. Consumers were moving away from buying manufacturers' branded goods that were traditionally bought from large department stores, small local outfitters or by mail order. Instead they preferred smaller, more 'exclusive' brand ranges created by the retailers themselves and the manufacturers' brands fell from favour. Much of the company's future manufacturing success, or otherwise, would depend on the successful winning of orders from the retail giants.

1964.

Symingtons step out for spring in Bri-nylon with a range of black nylon lace garments including this deep strapless bra from the Liberty range.
Its pre-formed cups were a product of the recently introduced moulding process which meant that bra shapes could be made using less complicated pattern pieces and shorter production time.

Museum ref. (J)
Consumer literature

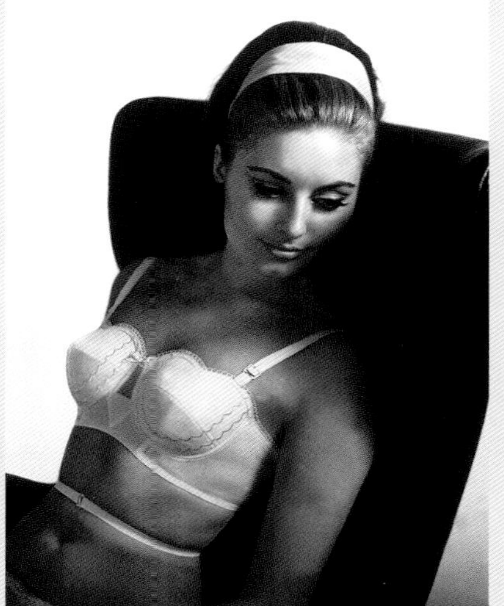

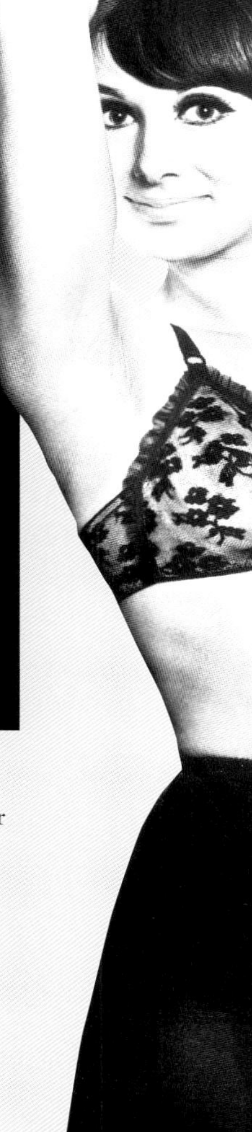

1964-1970.

By the middle of the 1960s the bra had become the staple foundation wear product for both manufacturers and customers. Control, shaping and support for the bust was all important and a wide variety of styles were made available to a market of diverse ages and figure types. Sizing became more and more sophisticated and accurate. These three bras show brief, medium and deep styles in a variety of colours and fabric treatments.

1. 1966.

Pull-on corset using the newly introduced 'Elura' a figured two way power lace to enhance its smooth line. The straps are detachable to allow for strapless wear, the nylon lace bra cups are under-wired and are lined with nylon voile. There is spiral steel boning running down each side of the garment.

Museum ref. J33

2. 1967.

A sleek pull-on girdle in stretch tricot made from elastomeric and nylon. This typifies the new fabrics that were emerging for use in the foundation garment industry, here creating a garment that achieved all of the functions of a traditional corset but without the boning, panelling, lace adjustment and bulky closures of earlier periods.

Museum ref. J43 (Bra J235)

3. 1968.

A bra slip with a supported bust line in multi-shades of blue nylon tricot. The cups of this bra slip are lined with foam rubber to give a full and smooth effect to the bust. The range was produced in shades of orange, blue, pink and yellow.

Museum ref. J23

4. 1968.

The *'New Magic Mist'* pantie corselet in white jacquard elastomeric net with an inner control panel for the stomach. The bra cups are lined with Fibrefil (polyester wading) to give an easy care smooth contour to the bust. The pantie corselet was designed to be worn with tights and therefore required no suspenders.

Museum ref. J119

5. 1968.

Long leg, strapless pantie corselet in black nylon elastomeric net. It has decorative lace panelling and power lace leg grips, which prevented the long legs from riding up. The cups of the bra are lined with Fibrefil to give a smooth outline to the bust.

Museum ref. (J)
Trade literature

6. 1979.

This deep pantie girdle is made from blended elastane power net and features a smooth, built in leg grip to prevent the long legs of the girdle riding or rolling up the leg.

Museum ref. K74

c1965.

A black and red Bri-nylon slip from the Eros Christmas range. Softer underwear was, by now being produced alongside the more structured foundation garments. Alcock and Priestly Ltd. were a subsidiary distribution company of Symington.

Museum ref. (J) Trade literature

1969.
'Gabriella' bra and pantie girdle in pink and orange flower print nylon. Matching sets of underwear became very popular in the 1960s and extended to a full range of named styles such as *'Lolita'*, *'Lana'*, *'Lucille'* and *'Apache'*.
Museum ref. (J) consumer literature

1968.

Peter Pan bra by Oleg Cassini, the designer who dressed Jackie Kennedy, and made under licence in Britain by Symington. The range was quite exclusive, a bra retailing at 3 guineas, but the styling and colours, including creme-de-menthe and burgundy, were seductive.

Museum ref. (H) Consumer literature.

V11 nylon lace bra with removable foam 'uplift', stretch-to-fit cups and straps in white, creme de menthe and burgundy. 3 guineas.

as advertised

great foundations at mean little prices

Eros meenies

1969.

Eros Meenies co-ordinates including *'pirouette'* a boy-leg pantie girdle in pale blue and *'Maytime'* a support brief in 'dolly print' Lycra.

Museum ref. J71a and J71c

Dressed For Success 1980-1990

Peony double-breasted swing coat with tie belt, worn with plum gabardine wide legged trousers. Modelled by Miss Linda Evangelista. Next Directory, Autumn / Winter 1989.

Reproduced by kind permission of Next Directory.

1987.

Lingerie designs by Neil Bultitude, who graduated from the BA Contour Course at Leicester Polytechnic (now DeMontfort University) and went straight to work at Symington. This design board shows the development of a small range of co-ordinating underwear along with samples of fabrics that were to be used.

The 1980s brought enormous changes to how women thought about their own bodies and the clothes that they put onto them. It was a decade of growth in the leisure industries, particularly in the field of exercise. Vast ranges of aerobic, dance and gym fashions were produced and exercise, whether it was at the gym or at home in front of a video, was the latest way of creating the fashionable female figure.

The high street shopping experience was also about to change. In 1982 Next opened its doors to reveal ranges of co-ordinating separates with high fashion styling at high street prices; the impact on other retailers was immediate and shopping trends began to change. Symington produced collections of underwear for Next, Marks and Spencer, Littlewoods and other high street leaders.

Underwear was no longer a foundation garment, it was pretty, decorative, sometimes sexy, comfortable and practical. In theory there was no need for figure controlling corsetry; a woman could achieve a perfect figure with a rigorous diet and exercise programme. Underwear reflected the new sporty mood with athletic styling, new stretch fabrics including Lycra were used extensively.

Bras, briefs and swimwear were the main production staples, but complete ranges of underwear, including camisoles, French knickers and slips were created by a team of young designers. These ranges were sold through high street chains and smaller independent retailers although much of Symington's production fed into the mail order market.

As the eighties came to an end the company faced the prospect of closure and redundancies and in May 1990 the factory finally closed.

For nearly one hundred and fifty years R. & W.H. Symington had produced corsetry and foundation wear for millions of women, at one point they operated more than twenty factories in five different countries.
They made the ideal figure of every change in fashion a reality for their female customers, they played their part in taking children out of corsets and their 'Peter Pan' swimsuits were worn by thousands of British holiday makers.

From Corset To Comfort

1920-25.
Plaster store display models of 'Soccer Sid the Liberty Kid' and 'Dashing Dora the Liberty Scorer'. These are just two of a wide range of plaster figures which were created to popularise the range amongst children, most of whom hated the Liberty Bodice.

1908.
The original advertising image for the Liberty Bodice shows Freda Cox, the daughter of Fred Cox, the Director of Symington who was responsible for the development and successful marketing of the Liberty Bodice.

The production of corsetry and stay bands for children appears to have been part of the Symington business from the late 1870s. By that time the practice of swaddling children in restricting bands of cloth had died out and young bodies were supported instead with stay bands or binders; flat panels of cloth that wrapped around the stomach and fastened with straps. These stay bands were believed to support the infant's body and prevent any deformity to the spine. They were usually made of cotton, interlined with hessian and corded or quilted at the back and front. The stay band had straps and ties that passed through slots in the side seams and fastened at the front.

Most children wore stay bands until around the age of eight, when girls would begin to wear specially designed corsets. There are several examples of corsets for young girls in the collection and their design reflects the figure requirements for the age of the wearer. Almost all the corsets feature adjustable elements such as buttoned or buckle shoulder straps which would allow for growth and development in a child's body.

Corsets designed for teenage girls featured pleated or gored bust sections and had small panels let into the skirts for the hips. There was little or no attempt to create a small or defined waist, the emphasis was on supporting and controlling the body. Many of the teenage corsets have a series of buttons arranged in a diamond pattern on each of the side seams. These buttons were attached to other pieces of underwear and were used in the following way: top button, for holding up a petticoat, two side buttons for the front and back of buttonholed drawers, bottom button for suspender looped stockings.

Social changes in ideas about childhood eventually led to the decline in the popularity of corsets for girls. In 1908 R. & W.H. Symington introduced the Liberty Bodice, which would finally take the place of girlhood corsets and stay bands.

The Liberty Bodice is R. & W.H. Symington's most famous product, either loved or loathed by generations of children born before the 1950s. When it was launched in 1908 it was a small revolution in the clothing of children, providing warmth, comfort and support without the stiffness of the corsets that it replaced. The garment was very simple, consisting of a button fastening, sleeveless bodice that was reinforced with cloth strapping running down the font and back panels and along the side seams.

The strapping gave gentle support to the body and kept the Liberty Bodice in shape even after laundering. There were buttons at the side seams so that stockings and drawers could be attached.

The Liberty Bodice was a great success and a whole department was given over to its making, at its height producing over 3,000,000 garments a year. The bodice was the brainchild of Frederick Cox the Marketing Director at Symington and the advertising, marketing and artwork for it was some of the most successful that the company produced. From the very beginning there was a concerted marketing campaign that included displays in shops and at trade fairs, press advertisements, specially commissioned plaster figures and a series of booklets, games and 'give-aways' which immediately engaged with the child customer directly.

Liberty Bodice wearers were portrayed as happy, fun, slightly heroic children with names like 'Soccer Sid the Liberty Kid' and 'Climbing Clara'.

'Priscilla', who appeared in an advertisement in 1922 asked "I'se got a Liberty Bodice, have you ?" and went on to say how her Liberty Bodice made "play more enjoyable" and that "children of all ages grow more supple, romp better and are better in every way".

As well as speaking directly to children Cox also targeted the parents in the marketing campaign. The Liberty Bodice was sold as being "flexible, porous and hygienic", advertisements claimed that it "gives perfect support without restraint".
In 1938 one of the plaster display figures showed a mother owl and her family in their roost, each one wearing a Liberty Bodice and accompanied by the slogan "Wise Mothers buy Liberty Bodices".

From 1908 until the end of the 1940s when its popularity began to decline the campaign in the media was tireless. The Liberty Bodice continued to be developed and changes were made throughout the years of its production. The original buttons, of which there were ten, were made of rubber; these were later replaced with plastic ones.
As children stopped wearing button-fastening stockings and drawers the buttons at the side seams were removed.

Production of the children's Liberty Bodice stopped in 1974 when world demand finally ceased.

c1880.

Baby's stay band of double lined red sateen bound with pale yellow. The stiffening for the bodice is created with an overall quilting of petal shaped stitching. The tightness of the stay band is adjusted with the wrap around strap. The shoulder straps are not adjustable.

Museum ref. AA1

c1880.

Girl's corset of beige and grey heavy jean, interlined with hessian and stitch corded. The corset has a front busk fastening and laces down the back. There are small bust and hip gores but the focus of the garment are the panels of cording which control the shoulders, back and stomach.

Museum ref. AA14

c1885.

Stay band of red sateen, corded vertically in a central panel for extra support.

Museum ref. AA3a

1895-1900.

Young girl's corset bodice in red sateen. Button fastening at the centre front and back lacing. The sides and centre front are corded for support and the shoulder straps are adjusted with buttons. There are small gored inserts for the bust.

Museum ref. AA4b

1895-1900.

Adolescent girl's corset with busk front fastening and partial lacing to the centre back. Two wide spiral steels support the cross-over back and shoulder pieces which fasten to the front bust sections with metal buckles. The support and shaping is created with string cording in vertical and diagonal panels.

Museum ref. AA6c

c1895.

Girl's *'Freedom Bodice'* in white double twill, corded all over and with a hessian interlining. The centre closes with five buttons and there are attachments for buttonhole drawers or stockings at the sides. Six diagonally corded panels flare the hip area.

Museum ref. AA5a

c1900.

Stay band in blue-grey herringbone cotton coutil, with corded panels front and back and a tie adjusting waistband.

Museum ref. AA9

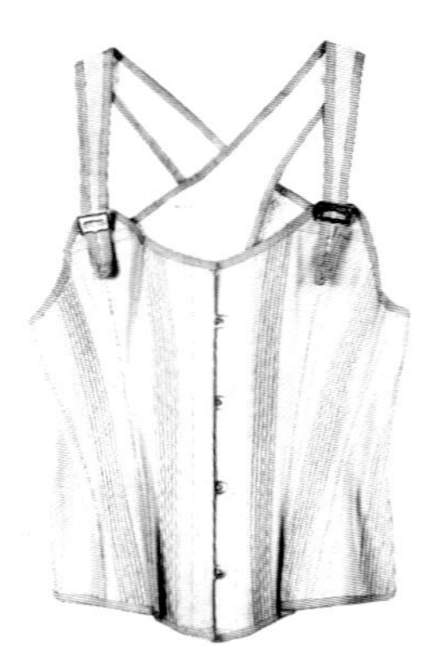

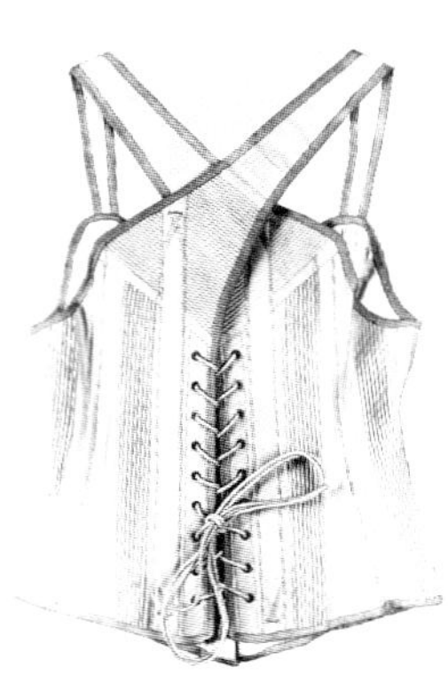

c1910.

Printed advertising card for the woven version of the Liberty Bodice. Fred Cox's marketing department rose to the challenge of the new product and created a range of advertising images which always featured happy, healthy, active children enjoying wearing their Liberty Bodices.

c1920.

The collection contains a large number of original artwork for advertisements and retailers' show-cards, which were produced by the marketing department. They show a child's fantasy world called 'Libertyland' where sweets grow on trees and teddy bears come to life and play with the children.

1905.

Girl's suspender bodice made from white cotton coutil, lightly corded and with button front fastening. There are side buttons for fastening onto buttonhole drawers. The two, very long suspenders are made from cotton tape and have closures of wire loops and rubber buttons.

Museum ref. AA13 (2)

1906.

Girl's button through bodice in quilted, unbleached knitted cotton. The forerunner of the Liberty Bodice this garment gave support, freedom of movement, comfort and warmth.

Museum ref. AA12 (1)

1907.

Corset bodice in white cotton twill with a button front fastening. The strappings, which run diagonally across the bodice, are similar to those of the Liberty Bodice, which was introduced the following year.

Museum ref. AA13 (4)

Printed box top from the original Liberty Bodice of 1908, showing an image from an Edwardian beach holiday.

c1925.

Porky the Porcupine enjoys wearing his Liberty Bodice in this newspaper advertisement which includes an early retailing 'offer' of a free set of dominoes in return for coupons from a Liberty Bodice.

Porky never gets cross now

"You can't put your spines up, Porky," said the Liberty Kids. "No," replied the Porcupine, "I'm never cross now I wear a Liberty Bodice, so I don't need to. I'm always so contented and comfy—I can romp and play to my heart's content.

Children are always happy in a "Liberty" Bodice, because it allows complete freedom of movement, and gives perfect support in any position. No restraint. Made of porous, knitted fabric. Hygienic and flexible. For children, growing girls and ladies. In white and natural.

(Knitted Fabric)

PRICES.

Infants', 1/11½; Children's, 1 to 3 yrs., 2/6; 4 to 8 yrs., 3/-; 9 to 13 yrs., 3/6; Young Ladies', 4/11; Large and O.S., 5/11. Ladies', 6/11; Large and O.S. 7/11; Knickers for Children up to 4 yrs., 2/3; Knickers in de luxe quality, 2/6.

FREE.—*CHILDREN'S DOMINOES. Send 2d. in stamps or the coupon off a "Liberty" Bodice for free set of children's dominoes.*

"LIBERTYLAND" (Dept. 63), MARKET HARBOROUGH.

1. 1908.

The original Liberty bodice in unbleached knitted cotton with herringbone weave cotton strappings and bone buttons. At the height of its popularity Symington was producing over 3 million Liberty Bodices every year.

Museum ref. AA12 (2)

2. 1910.

Adolescent girl's corset in dove sateen with button fastening at the centre front and lacing at the centre back. The bust sections are pleated and there are built up areas at the front of the shoulders where the straps fasten. This allows for some depth to the centre front which is decorated with a small strip of lace. The buttons at the side of the corset allow for fastening drawers, petticoats and stockings.

Museum ref. AA7b

3. 1916.

Stay band in white double cotton batiste lined with double wadding.
The stiffening is created with the diamond pattern of quilting. There are small stars embroidered in pale blue at the centre of each diamond. The waistband and shoulder straps adjust by the means of blue satin ribbons. The stay band is still in its original green leather wallet, which was carried by Symington salesmen when visiting retailers.

Museum ref. AA11b

4. 1917.

Stay band in white cotton interlined with stiff card and wadding. It has stiff, button adjustable shoulder straps, which cross at the centre back. The use of card is unusual but is probably due to wartime shortages of other more traditional stiffening and support materials.

Museum ref. AA11n

5. 1926.

Quilted stay band in white cotton batiste interlined with double wadding. Originally designed in 1916 this model was finally withdrawn in 1930.

Museum ref. AA11k

6. 1960.

Peter Pan Liberty Bodice in white fleecy fabric introduced in 1927.
The fleece replaced the original knitted cotton fabric in the mid 1930s and remained in production until 1974.

Museum ref. AA12 (8)

Taking The Plunge

1939.
Peter Pan beach outfit comprising a sun-suit of bra and shorts (which are joined at the centre back) shoulder cape and pointed cap all in leopard print rayon with 'multi-lactron' elastication.

c1950.
This advertising artwork is for one of the famous ***'Peter Pan'*** telescopic swimsuits that were made in a range of fabrics including cotton and nylon. The swimsuits came in a huge variety of colours and patterns. The telescopic shaping made one size fit virtually all figure types and the swimsuit kept its shape even when wet.

c1938.
Jungle print fabric swatches in different colourways for the children's swimwear range *'Junior Swimlette'*.

1938-39.
The *'Peter Pan'* range of swim and sports suits featuring beach outfits, swimming costumes and sun suits in a variety of fabric treatments and styles including one and two piece costumes.

1955.
Retailer's information booklet illustrating men's swimming trunks from the Peter Pan range made from elastic batiste. The colour range included black, royal blue, kingfisher blue and hot coral.

Sea bathing, long recognised as a healthy activity, reached the height of its popularity in the late Victorian period. Voluminous, body covering bathing dresses for women and suits for men were created to protect the wearer's modesty. These were usually made of wool or cotton and when wet, became heavy and clung to the body in deep folds. They were not intended for swimming in, as bathing was simply the immersion of the body in water and not an active, physical movement through it.

By the early years of the twentieth century lighter weight bathing and swimming costumes made from cotton jersey were designed to fit closer to the body and allowed for the possibility of active movement in the water. Knitted cotton and fine wool were still the most popular fabrics but they sagged very badly when wet.

Bathing styles, like everyday clothes, became briefer during the 1920s and by the early 1930s there was a demand for beach outfits that revealed more and more of the body in order to achieve the newly-fashionable sun tan.

In 1937, recognising a new and potentially profitable market, Frederick Cox encouraged the company to design and make a range of 'corset tailored sports suits' under the brand name 'Peter Pan'. Symington entered into a development agreement with Martin White Ltd and registered a patent for a 'telescopic' swimsuit. Lactron (cotton covered rubber) thread was stitched in narrow rows onto the inside of a fabric while being kept at a constant tension, the result was a circular ruched fabric with tremendous stretch. The fabric was made up into swimsuits of one size, which stretched to fit any figure ranging from size 8 to 18. The fit was nearly perfect and the swimsuit kept its shape even when wet. The ruched 'Peter Pan' swimsuit became a part of nearly every woman and child's holiday packing and remained popular until new fibre technology and new designs emerged in the 1950s.

In 1964 nylon stretch jersey was introduced into the Symington swimwear collections. It had stretch without the need for elastic, but it required the skills of a corset designer, pattern cutter and assembler to make a successful garment.

The Symington operatives were certainly skilled and the company produced very successful collections including bikinis, one-piece swimsuits in a range of styles for different figure types, swimming trunks for men and swimsuits for children, all in a wide variety of richly coloured and patterned fabrics.

By 1971 Du Pont had successfully introduced Lycra into swimwear fabrics, leading to improvements in the fit, stretch and shape retention of garments. Symington produced swimwear and beach outfits throughout the 1970s and 1980s, supplying the ever increasing market of package holiday sun worshippers and women who turned to swimming as part of their exercise regimes.

Ibiza holiday for
EROS

1969.

Psychedelic prints and colours for swimsuits and bikinis from the Eros range. By the beginning of the 1970s the package holiday had put Mediterranean beaches within relatively easy reach of thousands of holiday makers and fashionable beach and swimwear became an essential summer purchase.

1964.
'Nehru' one of the beach outfits from the Eros range of beach and swimsuits which was the staple of the Symington swimwear production of the mid 1960s. 'Nehru' was available in black, yellow and topaz and retailed for around £12.

1954.
Two swimsuits, on the left in red rayon for the younger figure and on the right in red and white check with boning at the sides and beneath the bust for greater support for a fuller figure. Swimwear had to fit and support in the same way as a foundation garment, but it also had to be lightweight and suitable to go into the water.

How Corsets Were Made

An afternoon visit to the corset factory, 1916

In 1916, a journalist from The London and Counties Journal paid a visit to R. & W.H. Symington and recorded in words and pictures, the different departments of the factory. Here are a selection of photographs from his visit, and his original captions that take us step by step through the process of making a corset. Below each caption is a description of the work of some of the different departments.

1. Cutting Room 2

"The various parts of the corset are first cut out from a series of wooden pattern pieces using a band knife that cuts through fifty or sixty layers of material with amazing ease. There are many of these band knives at Symington's each in the hands of a skilled cutter."

There were three cutting rooms at the factory, each producing thousands of pattern pieces every day. Patterns were scaled for different sizes and the band knife process meant that many pieces of fabric could be cut out at one time. The workbenches in the hand cutting rooms, which did more difficult or better quality work, had brass bound slots cut at standard angles which were used to allow the knives to cut through the layers of material. From the cutting room the corset pieces were passed to the sorters, who sorted and checked all of them before they were sent to the stitching room.

1.

2. Stitching Department

"There are several stitching machine rooms at Messrs Symington and they present happy and striking pictures of feminine activity. The cleanliness in the appearance of the place and the people is accentuated by the girls all wearing white overalls. This is done with the object of keeping the work spotless. The stitching is done rapidly and perfectly by power-driven single and multiple needle sewing machines."

All the corsets were stitched by machine and the sewing rooms were enormous to cope with the volume of production. All the sewing processes, including the fitting of boning and busks, were done in the stitching departments.

2.

3. Trimming Room

"The fine and delicate embroidery and lace trimming that go to make a corset a thing of art and beauty are added by skilled and experienced girls who have been specially trained for the purpose."

Corsets were trimmed with lace, slotted with ribbon and had embroidery on the casings that held the boning.

3.

4. Handwork Department

"During its construction a single corset passes through an astonishing number of hands. The work performed by each having its own importance and degree of interest."

Even mass produced corsets required some hand finishing. This was done by skilled seamstresses in a separate department of the factory.

4.

5. Examining Room

"After being finished the corset passes to the examining room where every part is carefully checked."

Only after passing through this quality control could a corset be packed and sent to the retailers.

5.

6. Boxing Up

"After being examined the corset is packed into its own box and a specially printed label bearing its name is pasted to the lid."

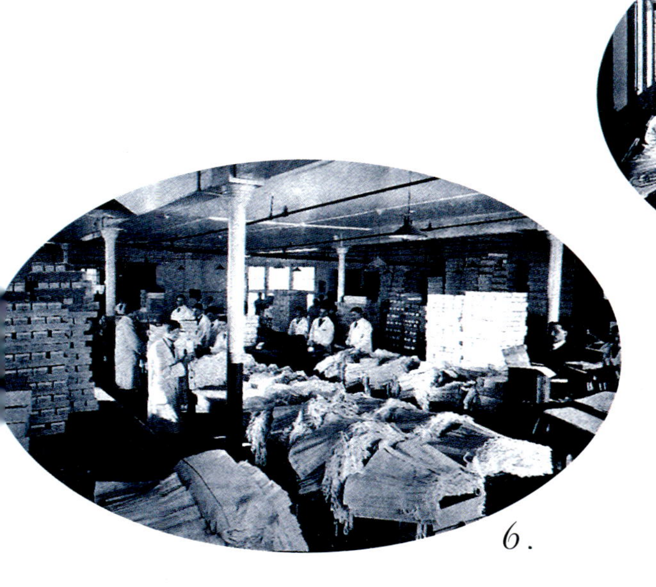

6.

7. Box Making Department

"The main factory has one section set apart from the rest, completely equipped with the latest machinery. Here are made all the cardboard corset boxes and everything in connection with the packaging of a corset for sale."

R. & W.H. Symington kept all elements of production under its own control, including the packaging in which the corsets were sold.

8. Printing Department

"There is also a printing department with letter press machines, type cases etc and the firm design and print their own labels for their customers, even to the tapes on the inside of the corsets."

Printed box tops, end labels and the small paper labels with sizing information that were fixed into the insides of the corset were all produced in the printing department. Decorative box tops were important parts of the selling process, the more attractive the box, the more likely the customer was to select it from a wide range of similar garments.

9. The Boiler House

"The firm have their own generating plant. The whole of the factories are lighted, and the machines driven, by electricity. The boiler house is fitted with large Lancashire Boilers supplying heat and water for the laundry, for Messrs Symington have everything washed and laundered on the premises."

7.

8.

9.

The Art Of Corset Making

A late nineteenth century corset was made up in the following way. The pattern was cut out of three different sorts of fabric, a facing cloth, a hessian interlining and a cotton lining. The corset pieces were sewn together and boning stitched into 'casings' that lay on the top of the facing cloth. These casings were often finished with decorative stitching called flossing. The stitching, including areas of quilting for shape and support passed through all three layers of the corset. (By the early 1880s the hessian interlining was generally abandoned in favour of other methods of stiffening such as steam moulding, quilting and cording.)

A busk fastening of metal, which closes with a number of studs and loops, was added at the centre front.

At the centre back two rows of eyelets were punched for the lacing. Lacing a corset meant that the fit could be adjusted to emphasise different parts of the figure and so that a mass-produced, ready to wear garment could achieve some accuracy of fit. It was usual to lace the corset to the middle from both the top and bottom, giving the greatest support to the waist.

When a corset was ready to be finished it was taken to the copper block room in the factory where lines of hollow copper forms were attached to a steam heating mechanism. The corset was laced onto the forms and brushed with cold wet starch. The steam inside the form heated the copper and set the starch and the corset was moulded into its final and permanent shape.

Boning

Whalebone had been used in the making of stays and bodices for centuries, it was lightweight, flexible and could be split into thin strips. The whaling industries of North America, Britain, Russia, Japan and many Scandinavian countries were enormous but despite the slaughter of thousands of whales the supply of whalebone was never limitless. The price fluctuated constantly and as a result manufacturers could never be assured of a reliable supply. As early as the eighteenth century steel, wood and cane were being used as a substitute for whalebone.

There were other ways of boning garments. By the middle of the 1870s American corsetiers were using buffalo horn, but as the American Buffalo was being hunted to near extinction the supply could not be guaranteed.

Dried and processed reeds were also used in the boning process, different types were used under the generic term 'split cane'. The cane had all the properties of bone and horn but with the added advantage of being able to be pierced by the sewing needle. This meant that decorative embroidery could be applied over boning. The canes were approximately 1cm wide and were inserted in strips between vertical rows of stitching.

By the late 1880s boning of whatever kind was applied to the outside of the corset in single casings and these were decorated with embroidery and overstitching.

Throughout the nineteenth century there had been experiments in the successful use of steel for boning in garments. Certainly the metal could be made into lightweight strips but early attempts could not produce the suppleness required and rusting after laundry was a continuing problem.

Perhaps the earliest corset in the collection successfully to exploit all the potentials of steel boning is an American corset from 1895 (Museum ref. B32a). The rust proof steels are light and slim and were pre-formed so that the corset maintains its perfect shape at all times.

By the beginning of the twentieth century flat steels were being universally used in the corsetry industry. In 1907 the 'Spirella' corset company introduced 'spiral' steels, these were made from flat spirals of thin steel. These steels were much more flexible and had movement both sideways as well as forward and back and, by the 1920s were used by almost all the corsetry manufacturers.

Cording

Cording was a popular method of giving suppleness to a garment whilst still allowing the figure to be controlled. It made corsets hard wearing and, because it did not use metal parts, made them easier to launder.

Cotton or Stitch Cording

Cotton cording is created by tramlines of stitching of varying widths that pass through all three layers of the fabric of the corset. The rows of stitching gave support to the fabric and the direction of the rows could be altered to shape the garment. The sewing machines could stitch through the layers of fabric with relative ease and the cording method meant that more expensive whalebone could be reserved for areas of the corset that required more rigid and defined support.

Cane Cording

Cane cording used the fibres of the Mexican ixtle plant to make a form of support that was supple and almost unbreakable. In 1885 the American company Warner Brothers patented the machinery which could transform the raw ixtle fibres into a cording material called Coraline. Coraline was used by Symington from the middle of the 1880s and there are four corsets in the collection which are corded using the process (A41 is a good example). The material was expensive to import and was gradually replaced by less expensive string cording.

String Cording

At the end of the 1870s Symington began to manufacture some corsets which had no hessian interlining. Instead thin strips of hemp twine were threaded into the channels created by the cording stitches. This was done by hand using a 45cm needle which was specially designed for the purpose. When the corset was being finished the ends of the twine were cut off and the open edges of the corset closed and bound.

By the middle of the 1880s the heavy hemp cording was replaced by lighter weight twine made from paper, which was cut and wound onto reels so that it could be twisted into cord. The paper was machine twisted as it passed through water and dye which gave it strength and colour. Different plys of paper were used to cord different sorts of corset which required greater or lesser support and shaping.

Special sewing machines were adapted to carry out the string cording. A unit of around ten machines was grouped on a raised platform in the workroom. The needle plates of the machines overhung the edge of the stand so that there was a drop of around 2 metres between the plate and the floor. A raised walkway for the machine operators surrounded the platform. The facing cloth and the lining were cut to the required width and usually in lengths of around 4 metres. The string cording was fed between the two fabrics from an overhead bobbin. The ends were joined together and fed through the sewing machine as a double looped band. The string was then stitched in continuous rows between the two cloths. Because of the gap below the needle plate there was no risk that the fabric would touch the workroom floor. (See above photograph.)

Glossary

Avro: Symington brand name used between the 1920s and the early 1980s.

Band knife: Power driven knife used to cut multiple layers of fabric.

Bandeau: Form of brassière which closes at the side or back made from strips of fabric or panels of elasticated or knitted fabric with minimal shaping, used to flatten rather than support the bust.

Barmen edging: Bands of woven tape of varying widths used to construct panels or sometimes whole sections of corsets.

Batiste: A fine, sheer plain weave cotton or polyester fabric.

Boning: Narrow strips of material usually cane, bone or steel stitched into a garment to give shape and support.

Brassière: The forerunner of the bra this was the name given to a variety of different garments that controlled, shaped and supported the bust.

Bri-nylon: Brand name for nylon manufactured by I.C.I. Fibres Ltd.

Broche: Silk, cotton or later rayon fabric with a satin surface pattern woven on a jacquard loom.

Broderie Anglaise: All white cotton embroidery, usually of floral design incorporating small holes mainly worked in satin and buttonhole stitches.

Busk: The piece of stiffening material, usually whalebone, wood or metal, inserted into the front of the corset to keep it braced against the curves of the body. The busk later became the method for fastening the corset at the front.

Busk-front: The front fastening of a corset using interlocking metal parts. The method of closing the corset gave its name to any corset design with a centre-front stud and loop closure.

Bust improver: Garment designed to change the shape and size of the bust, worn over a corset and beneath a bodice or blouse.

Cambric: Fine white linen, and later cotton, used extensively in underwear production.

Casing: Strips of fabric attached to the outside of garments into which the boning was slotted.

Circle stitched: Continuous spiral stitches that radiate around the cups of a brassière to give support and shape to the bust.

Coraline: Trade name given to the processed cane from the ixtle plant used in cane cording, developed by the Warner Brothers Company in USA.

Cording: Method of giving support and shape to a corset by sewing through the layers of fabric to produce narrow parallel lines of stitching.

Corselet: A garment combing the functions of a brassière and a girdle. A garment with shoulder straps, bra section and skirted abdominal control usually with attached stocking suspenders.

Corset: A stiffened garment that supported and shaped the torso. For the period of Symington's production it was typically front fastening and back lacing.

Coutil: Firm twilled cotton, or later cotton and rayon fabric, closely woven in herringbone construction.

Crêpe de Chine: Silk fabric with a smooth back and a slightly wrinkled surface.

Elastane: The European term for the group of synthetic elastomeric fibres such as Lycra and Spanzelle, which were known as Spandex in the USA.

Elastic: Threads of rubber encased in silk or cotton.

Eros: Brand name used by Symington beginning in the 1960s.

Fibrefil: Polyester wadding used in bra cups to give a smooth outline to the bust.

Flossing: Decorative stitching used to close the casings on the outside of a corset and to anchor the boning in place.

Girdle: Lightweight corset that controlled the waist and upper thighs usually rubberised or elasticated and with attached stocking suspenders.

Health belt: A garment that resembles a short girdle or a deep suspender belt. The health belt controlled the abdomen, buttocks and upper thighs but allowed a certain degree of freedom of movement.

Hessian: Strong, coarsely woven cloth made from hemp or jute. In its finer gauge weave it was used as an interlining for corsets.

Ixtle: Mexican reed plant used as a raw material for cane cording.

Lactron elastication: Used in swimsuits during the 1930s and 1950s, a method of giving full elastication and stretch to a tubular garment by sewing elasticated fibres onto the inside of a fabric whilst both thread and fabric are held under tension.

Lastex: 1931 Trade name for strips of rubber covered with silk, cotton, wool or rayon to form a yarn. Introduced by the US Rubber Co.

Lasting: A durable cloth of twisted yarn.

Leaver's Lace: Machine made lace, named after John Leavers its inventor.

Liberty Bodice: Fleecy bodice with reinforcing tapes introduced for children in 1908 and adults in 1912.

Liberty: Brand name for garment ranges from the mid 1930s until 1990.

Locknit: The knitted form of rayon.

Lycra: Synthetic elastomeric fibre with stretch and recovery properties. Invented by Du Pont USA in 1959 and launched in Britain in 1960.

NuBack: Registered trade name for an elasticated panel inserted into the back of a girdle or corselet, which prevented the garment from riding up at the back. First introduced in 1932 it remained in use until the 1970s.

Nylon: The first synthetic fibre, a polyamide developed by the Du Pont laboratory in 1938, in both its knitted or woven from it was used extensively in underwear production.

Peter Pan: Brand name first given to Symington's swimwear range in the 1930s, extended to underwear in the 1950s.

Polyester: A synthetic fibre, with good washing properties, first developed in 1941 by the Calico Printers association laboratory in Lancashire.

Power net: Any net fabric that has added elastication used in panels on girdles, corselets and bras.

Princess line: The name given to the construction of dresses and bodices without a waist seam.

Quilting: Stitching through multiple layers of fabric to give added stiffness and support and also to produce decorative patterns on the surface of a garment.

Rayon: The name given to artificial silk, a manmade fibre made of regenerated cellulose using chemical wood pulp. Developed commercially by Courtaulds from 1905.

Sateen: Cotton fabric with a glossy surface.

Selvedge: The woven edge of cloth created so that it cannot fray or unravel.

Spiral steel: Introduced by Marcus Merrit Beeman of the Spirella Company of Pennsylvania these were lightweight and flexible steel bones for use in foundation garments.

Stay band: A child's garment that wraps around the upper torso fastening with ties at the front. Usually quilted or stiffened the stay band was supposed to support the infant's body in early development.

Stays: C17th and C18th term for a boned under-bodice, later known as a corset.

String cording: A method of supporting a corset using paper twine inserted between rows of stitching.

Swami: Knitted rayon with a glossy surface, used in bra production during the 1930s.

Terylene: The brand name given to the first polyester fibre discovered in 1941 the production of which was taken over by I.C.I. Fibres Ltd.

Tricot: Fine gauge knitted fabric.

Velcro: Fastening using two panels, one of which has tiny hooks the other has multiple long, soft, loops which attach to each other when closed and open by being torn apart.

Voile: Semi-transparent cloth of cotton, wool or silk, and later synthetic fibres.

Wraparound: A short girdle that closed by having a panel that wrapped over the front section and fastened at the side.

Acknowledgments & Further Reading

Anon. In Our Own fashion: The Story of R. & W. H. Symington & Co., Ltd. (Harley Publishing, 1956)

Carter, Alison, Underwear, The Fashion History (Batsford, 1992)

Colmer, Michael, From Whalebone to See Through: A History of Body Packaging (Cassell Australia Ltd., 1979)

Cox, Caroline, Lingerie: A lexicon of Style (Scriptum Editions, 2000)

Cunnington, C.W. & P., The History of Underclothes (Michael Joseph, 1951; rev. edn. Faber, 1991)

Ewing, Elizabeth, Dress and Undress: A History of Women's Underwear (Batsford, 1978)

Levitt, Sarah, Victorians Unbutton'd: Registered Designs for Clothing, their Makers and Wearers, 1839-1900 (Allen & Unwin, 1986)

Martin, Richard, Infra Apparel (Metropolitan Museum of Art/Abrams, New York, 1993)

Newman, Karoline; Proctor, Gillian; Bressler, Karen, A Century of Lingerie (Quarto Books, 1998)

Page, Christopher, Foundations of Fashion: The Symington Collection of Corsetry 1856-1979 (Leicestershire Museums, 1981)

Taylor, Lou & Wilson, Elizabeth, Through the Looking Glass: A History of Dress from 1860 to the Present Day (BBC Books, 1989)

Tobin, Shelley, Inside Out; A brief History of Underwear (The National Trust, 2000)

Waugh, Norah, Corsets and Crinolines (Batsford, 1964)

Articles

Mactaggart, P. & R. A., Half a Century of Corset Making: Mrs. Turner's recollections (Costume, 11,1979)

Mactaggart, P. & R. A., Ease, Convenience & stays, 1750-1850 (Costume 13, 1981)

The garment and archive photographs in this publication were taken by Steve Thursfield, Catherine Lines and Roger Rixon.

All images, with the following exceptions, are from the Symington collection and are the copyright of Leicestershire County Council Museums, Arts and Records Service.

Pages 11, 15, 44, 51, 56 from a private collection; page 52 reproduced by kind permission of The Berlei archive; page 65 reproduced by kind permission of The Woolmark; page 72 with thanks to Next Directory.

Since 1980 successive staff of Leicestershire Museums, Arts and Records Service have cared for the Symington Collection. Special acknowledgement is due to Pam Inder, Annette Carruthers, Jane May, Paula Waite, Amber Rowe, Fiona Graham, Steph Mastoris, Lindsay Souster, Sarah Williams and the late Eileen Nicholson.

The Museum Service is grateful for the support of a dedicated team of volunteers; those who have freely given their time to work with the Symington collection include Rod Quilter, Alison Smith, Julia Cox, Maureen Kent and Barbara Hallam.

My personal thanks are due to Gillian Proctor of Nottingham Trent University and to Valerie Steele of the Museum at FIT, New York, for their enthusiasm for the collection and this publication. Thanks also to John Mathias and Eleanor Thomas for reading the text and to Ken Stone for being calm throughout it all.

My final thanks go to Ian Jones of the Central Design Unit for his skill and creativity in making this book.

Philip Warren

Index

There is no sub-divided index entry for R. & W.H. Symington & Co. Ltd.